The Ideal Enterprise

Managing by the "Law of the Sphere"
for maximum profitability

Hans D. Baumann

VANTAGE PRESS
New York

Published by Vantage Press, Inc.
516 West 34th Street, New York, New York 10001

Manufactured in the United States of America
ISBN: 0-533-14185-0

Library of Congress Catalog Card No.: 02-91560

0 9 8 7 6 5 4 3 2 1

Dedication

This book is dedicated to Peter H. Baumann, John T. Beaudouin, Catherine E. Brashear, Edward C. Cating, and my dear wife, Sigrid. This book would never have been completed without their help.

Contents

Introduction...v

Chapter 1.. 1

CHASING THE RAINBOW OR HOW TO GET STARTED
Leadership Qualifications   10
Legal Entanglements   13
How Much Starting Capital Do I Need? 14
How to structure your company 19
Do I need a Web Site?   22
How to find a financial angel   26
Finding the right location   29

Chapter 2.. 32

HOW TO MANAGE A COMPANY, OR HOW NOT TO FOLLOW
THE OLD RULES

Chapter 3.. 50

RULES FOR SUCCESSFUL MANAGEMENT

Chapter 4.. 53

INCENTIVES AND DISINCENTIVES

Chapter 5.. 62

ENTROPY AND OTHER HEADY STUFF

Chapter 6.. 67

MEETINGS, OR MANAGING BY COMMITTEE
Domestic Meetings   67
International Meetings   75
What to do about meetings.   78

Chapter 7 82

BUDGETS
How to establish a yearly operating budget   83
Planning for capital expenditures   88

Chapter 8 91

THE COMPUTER AND OTHER FORMS OF MISCOMMUNICATION
E-Mail Mania   92
Phone tag or other office fun   98
How to communicate effectively.   99
Data explosions 102

Chapter 9 108

COMPUTER SOFTWARE

Chapter 10 116

RUNNING AN ENTERPRISE GOVERNMENT STYLE

Chapter 11 126

WHY SMALLER IS BETTER
Scaling factors in nature 127
Scaling factors and business   131
Why is this happening? 138
Lessons to be learned   146

Chapter 12 149

THE LAW OF THE SPHERE
Law of the Sphere   166
How to reverse the process   178

Chapter 13 185

MERGERS AND AQUISITIONS
Bad Mergers   191

Chapter 14 202

HOW THE GOVERNMENT CAN HELP YOU

Chapter 15.. 209

WHAT DO THEY MEAN WHEN THEY SAY…
AN IRREVERENT GLOSSARY

Index 218

FOREWORD

What happens when firms grow? Do they become more or less efficient? More or less profitable? Who benefits from the growth? The owners? The managers? The employees? The public? For generations, business practitioners, political scientists, policymakers, economists and the general public have asked these questions.

At a public policy level, concerns about size leading to market power and to "monopoly" pricing have long informed U.S. antitrust policy. Lying behind these concerns are explicit or implicit assumptions that increases in firm size would eventually lead to monopoly profits for the owners - assumptions that rest on a positive correlation between size and profitability. But, if size, by itself, made it possible to eventually earn monopoly profits, why, in the absence of governmental regulation, don't we observe only one large firm in every industry? Or, in the extreme, one large company that does everything?

Actually, these last two questions are part of a strand of economic inquiry into why firms even exist instead of having every transaction take place in arms-lengths markets. In a nutshell, the usual answer is that eventually the benefits of forming and operating an

i

organization called the firm are offset by bureaucratic costs such as empire building, logrolling and allocating funds within the organization on the basis of personalities and politics rather than economic merit. But, how do we know when firms are "too large" or that they have organized themselves inefficiently? And, even if we did know, how could such outcomes be discouraged?

These are questions financial economists have been grappling with, especially during the last twenty-five years or so with the emergence of financial agency theory and free cash flow theories of corporate finance and governance. Both of these closely intertwined theories concern themselves with conflicts of interest among corporate stakeholders and, in particular, between managers and owners (the shareholders) of a company.

Free cash flow is defined as the cash remaining after all operating and financial charges, including debt repayments, as well as investments needed to maintain existing operations have been made. The "free cash" remaining can be used to make additional investments, pay down debt or distribute to the shareholders as cash dividends. Now, here is the crux of the matter. Given that managers are the agents (hired by) of shareholders who, in turn, want management to maximize the company's stock price (the present value of all future free cash flows), managers should only invest in profitable investments (technically defined as those investments that earn more than their cost of capital). But managers may be more inclined to run the company in their own best interests rather than that of the owners. Such behavior appears as growing the firm at the expense of profits because managerial compensation is correlated with the size of a company and the number of hierarchical layers and with increased consumption of perks such as first class air travel and corporate jets, yachts and golf club memberships. So, how do you discourage managers from doing this? Well, according to contemporary financial agency theory, you do the following:

You find ways to remove the free cash from control of the managers. One way is to substitute debt and lease financing for equity capital. Then, managers will be "forced" to use cash to pay down debt rather than make unprofitable investments. Another way is to distribute the cash as cash dividends to the shareholders. And, another way is to tie managerial and employee compensation to performance measured in terms of share price and long-term profitability metrics.

Hans D. Baumann, the founder of a very successful manufacturing company and an inventor with over 100 patents expresses these ideas very succinctly. As he puts it, "The purpose of a company is to make money, not to make or sell widgets."

What Hans Baumann offers us in The Ideal Enterprise are strategies he has successfully used to make money and, in the jargon of financial agency theory, to reduce, if not eliminate, the agency costs associated conflicts of interest between managers and owners.

Baumann has mathematically modeled how growth for growth's sake is likely to lead to a deterioration of profitability and the destruction of owner's wealth. The primary cause of this deterioration is the expansion of a managerial and staff (overhead) bureaucracy that chews up cash that otherwise could be used to pay cash dividends or invest elsewhere in better opportunities. In other words, Baumann has identified the principal agency costs and tells you how to control these costs.

Baumann's recommendations are practical and straightforward. Some may work better for some firms than others; but, more importantly, he offers a practical framework for starting and running your own business based on reducing overhead and increasing employee efficiency.

Oh yes. How do we know when firms have become "large"? Well, one sign is they have become unprofitable by making investments that fail to cover their cost of capital and, therefore, cause a misallocation of resources at an economy-wide level. Often, this occurs because of a corporate bureaucracy more interested in perpetuating itself than in anything else.

Fred R. Kaen
Professor of Finance
Whittemore School of Business and Economics
University of New Hampshire
Durham, NH (August 2001)

Introduction

Having started and operated my own successful company, I thought I should share my knowledge about how to properly organize a company and to have fun making profit in the process. Nothing contributes more to the stress level of a company leader than a *red* balance sheet. Losing money is no fun.

During my professional life and association with variously sized companies, I found that with increase in manpower the efficiency or, profitability as function of sales, would suffer. This fact bothered me and I tried to find out why. Perhaps there is a hidden Rule or Law, which could predict such an outcome. Taking a hint from nature, where scaling laws abound, I discovered that a similar relationship might apply for businesses. Hence, *The Law of the Sphere*. What this law implies is that profit may not necessarily increase in proportion to sales, or company size, but at a lesser, decreasing rate. This tends to make smaller companies more efficient than larger ones. Lest I be misunderstood, I am not against larger corporations because they definitely have a number of advantages.

What I try to point out in this book is that they could be much better organized for increased efficiency and certainly higher profit levels!

There are literally hundreds of business *guidebooks* or *how to manage* books around, so why write another one? My answer is, look at the authors. Most of them are consultants who have never run a successful business but who are clever at inventing new slogans. You have to wade through 200 or more pages propagating: *reengineering management*, one must have *vision*; you must call your employees *associates*; have *quality circles*; use *queuing theories,* have a *mission*; *shared values*; *do it right the first time (*I wonder why anybody would willfully do it the wrong way*?), develop team work, or* even better yet, use m*arket-disruptive analyses or supply chain integration.* This can be very confusing and will not help you learn how to motivate and reward your employees, organize your computer system, design a web site, spot wasteful fads, communicate with customers, staff non-productive departments, obtain financing, structure your company, and other very down to earth problems.

The proposed *Law of the Sphere* provides a mathematical tool to show you how profit rates can decrease with the increase in the number of supportive personnel (overhead), when companies grow. It also shows you how this relates to the number of reporting levels. This, in turn, could serve as a guide on how to structure your company or department in order to maintain or increase profitability.

All anecdotal information and tabulated data are based on facts with the sole exception of the probably classified data shown in chapter 10. Unless indicated otherwise, I did not state company names in order to protect the innocent.

The casual reader of this book may infer that I dislike computers. This is far from the truth. There are thousands of functions where computers are literally indispensable in our complex world. This manuscript was typed on one! What I do object to, and try to highlight, is the widespread misuse, or misapplication of computers and, even worse, software. That is what drains company profits and what decreases operating efficiency. Literally millions of dollars are wasted daily on wrong or unneeded software!

We have heard much good, but alas, also much hype about the *Internet*. Here are some thoughts on the subject. In order to gain the true perspective, ask yourself the question: Can the Internet create wealth? The answer is NO. In itself the Internet can create nothing despite all the IPO millionaires! It is only a communication tool much like, but superior to, the telephone or the mail. As a good tool and with proper usage, it can reduce office work and thereby increase profit by reducing overhead.

For example, if you do all your company purchases through the Internet that saves you man-hours and enables you to sell your widgets at a higher profit. However, the widgets themselves (your only wealth creation) are still done by machines in your factory!

One should realize that low profit levels in most companies are due to excess personnel, usually the non-productive type. Thomas Paine, in 1792 coined the phrase: *There are two distinct classes in the Nation, those who pay taxes and those that receive and live upon taxes.* We may expand on this by saying: *There are those who create wealth in a company and those who consume it.* Let's make sure that there are always more of the "creators" than of the "consumers" of profit in your business!

The recommendations laid down in this book may be unconventional, but have proven to be highly successful and, hopefully, will guide you to success in starting or running a company, a division, or department. When I may sound too negative at times, that certainly was not my intention. However, we can only learn to avoid the truly *negatives* by pointing out the foibles, the hype, the fads, and the waste that we all encounter in our daily jobs. If it takes ridicule to do the job, so be it.

I hope some budding entrepreneur or seasoned executives read this book and benefit from it. If, consequently, I can contribute to the economic well being of my country, then that shall be my reward.

So what is an *ideal enterprise*? It is a business that maximizes profit while requiring minimum capital and labor.

Chapter 1

CHASING THE RAINBOW OR HOW TO GET STARTED

Never confuse market research with wishful thinking.

Ever wondered about the lack of new technological developments? No, I am not talking about the latest improved software programs.

Consider jet planes for a minute. Their basic design was completed during World War II. What we see now is larger or faster versions of it. Consider television or tape recorders, both of which were developed 50 to 60 years ago. We keep improving designs such as using microprocessors instead of the vacuum tube, which gave us the chance to miniaturize electronic equipment and to run it faster, but it did not create any new basic technologies. Nothing yet has replaced the automobile as our principal mode of transportation. Rocket technology was developed in the 1920s and 1930s. Rockets have increased in size

1

and guidance systems have been improved, but that is all. Our common household appliances date back more than 80 years. Sure, we have more bells and whistles on a dryer, but that does not improve the basic method of drying our laundry! Radar was developed in the 1930s, and so it goes.

There are, of course, exceptions. For example, the more recent development of laser technology created a host of new products and enables us to use laser disk technology to vastly improve data storage and retrieval. Other areas are microchips and biotechnology. Software does abound and does astonishing things, even though, basic computer codes were developed in the 1960th. But compared to the period between 1930 and 1950, the progress is puny indeed.

Maybe it is a moot point to ask such questions about the lack of progress in the development of basic inventions, but I don't think so! The absence or low level of development of new technologies reflects a basic cultural change in our society. This void is not only restricted to sciences and technologies, but is also apparent in the lack of cultural achievements such as to outstanding writers (where is today's Steinbeck, Faulkner, or Hemingway?); great composers (No, I don't count the Grateful Dead!); and great painters (where are they?).

It is perhaps up to the philosophers to speculate on the origins of such a cultural malaise (which, on the other side of the coin, may contribute to negative effects

2

such as a high crime rate, higher teenage suicide rates, and to ongoing drug problems).

The explanation I prefer is: This is the result of a lack of challenge and, therefore, a lack of purpose. Primarily this is an undesirable by-product of our high standard of living. For the overwhelming majority of Americans, all the basic needs for food, clothing, and housing are fulfilled. Our most pressing problem seems to be deciding which one of the most exciting new movies we want to see.

Gone are the days of the Great Depression, a very good ` motivator indeed for our grandparents, and World War II and the Korean War for our parents. It is astounding to read the suicide statistics in times of war or famine, which were virtually *zero*! Back then, we were too busy trying to survive, so we had neither the time nor inclination to kill ourselves.

The particular cultural malaise I am talking about is not a new phenomenon. For example, it occurred in China during the middle of the second millennium, caused primarily by the teachings of Taoism as espoused by Lieh-Tzu in about 400 A.D. In the 18th century, the government under Tai Cheng more or less mandated the *do not question the laws of nature* philosophy, making research and development socially unacceptable. It also occurred in Europe after the fall of the Roman Empire, starting around 400 A.D. and lasting until the beginning of the Renaissance.

3

The way I see it, this cultural/technological malaise is the major cause of Japan's economic slump over the past ten years. We may blame this on the decrease in real-estate prices or the Japanese bank crisis, but these are only the effects of the underlying technological crisis, not the cause.

For the past 50 years, Japan has managed to exploit inventions made either in the United States or Europe and adroitly convert them into efficient and mostly low-cost consumer products. This strategy works as long as there were always new basic innovations waiting to be exploited. However, within the last 10 to 15 years, this particular well has dried up. There indeed may be a limit of how many improvements can be made on a camcorder or a CD player.

Even worse is that lesser-developed Asian countries now manufacture many of the same products as Japan, albeit at lower labor rates! This is a serious problem not only for Japan, but also for the western countries since we are so financially and economically intertwined.

The cure would be for the United States (and Europe) to again develop new, basic technologies such as the means to supplant the automobile or develop entertainment devices that gratify not only the eye and ear (as is done presently), but also the sense of smell and touch. Alas, inventions cannot be commanded by government grants nor by the monetary largess of a corporation. They mostly derive from the vision and hard work of individuals (much the same as artists do

4

their works). Unfortunately, there are now cultural roadblocks (as there were in Asia), which tend to prevent this from happening: (1) the lack of motivation (no empty stomach!); (2) the lack of education (consider the ratio of engineers to attorneys in the United States!); and, finally, (3) the fallacy of corporate managements to insist on doing research and development (meaning *inventing*) by teams only.

Pardon me for digressing. You may rightly ask, "what has this got to do with me becoming an entrepreneur interested in starting my own business?"

You may not realize it, but this affects you a lot. Since we cannot all be a Bill Gates, we have to be realistic. The lack of new technologies prevents exploiting new markets for new gadgets that the public would be eager to buy, thereby opening up new profit opportunities. Instead, like the majority of all businesses, you are forced to manufacture or sell *me-too* products, i.e., second-hand technology.

However, there are four ways to start your new business:

1. Purchase and use new and superior manufacturing techniques, thereby lowering costs and out-selling your competitor. A possibility, but somewhat remote. Chances are your competitor, who is also under price pressure, has thought of this already.

5

2. Reduce the quality of a product by using less expensive materials and/or fewer parts, thereby cutting costs. Not very ethical, but a widely practiced art in making a buck, or

3. If you are technically inclined, you can always redesign and improve the performance of an old technology. Consider how many times Sony Corp. has redesigned the good old tape recorder, each time with astonishing financial success. Redesigning and improving on old core technologies keeps 90% of all businesses going!

Mr. R.H. Jenrette[*] was only half right when he stated that when consultants say, "*return to your (old) core business*," corporate rigor mortis sets in. There are indeed still many ways to modify and live off such improved core business products that will keep you from going under!

4. Run a more efficient enterprise. Make a profit in a competitive environment by reducing overhead. The following chapters will show you how to do this.

However, before you decide to quit your job and become a budding capitalist, do your homework. Make a thorough marketing plan. Pick the product, study your competitors, and know their cost structure. Most importantly, know their weaknesses whether it is

---

[*] Richard H. Jenrette, *Jenrette's The Contrarian Manager*, (New York: McGraw-Hill, 1997).

cost, quality, performance, or delivery. Exploiting such weaknesses will get you started. Keep in mind that *wishful thinking is no substitute for a realistic marketing or product plan.*

Try to manufacture only a few, "standardized" product lines. By "standard' I mean products that have the least amount of variation in design and material, leading to the possibility of mass producing the given product with the resultant savings in inventory and production cost. Resist the call by your sales force to add "bells and whistles" to your standard products. While this may bring your sales representative a few more sales and, therefore, commissions, your bottom line will certainly suffer. Why? Because the "specials" will need extra attention not only in order entry, but also in Engineering, Planning, Procurement, and Assembly. This is additional cost that typically is not properly accounted for and which invariably affects your profit. When listening to the pleas of your sales representative, keep this in mind: his commission is the same whether or not *you* make a profit. There is a common goal between the manufacturer and his sales force; that is, to increase the sales volume. However, when it comes to making a profit, motives are diametrically opposed! Do not forget this at your peril!

There certainly are niche businesses that specialize in producing specialty products. With proper organization, these businesses can be profitable. However, never, ever combine the two, i.e., try to

7

manufacture "standard" and "special" products under one roof.

Next, make a very conservative financial forecast keeping in mind that there will not be one dime of profit coming in for at least one year (not counting several months of hard work before your company even starts). Don't rely on banks for financing. You probably don't have enough collateral (if you had it, you would not need the loan). The best starting capital is your own savings. The emotional attachment to your *own* money will keep you from buying an expensive company car, fancy furniture, or elaborate computer equipment. Second hand items will do quite well until the money starts flowing in. Here is your choice: do you want to have a positive cash flow, or do you want to impress your friends and neighbors?

Also important is whom you hire to support your enterprise. Cultivating good initial employees should start way before you get incorporated. These should be very talented and outstanding people. Knowing and observing them for many years will reveal their strengths and weaknesses. Remember, these initial employees will be your department managers when you start growing. For example, I have known the person who later became my vice president of sales for almost 20 years (when he still was a student) prior to engaging him. He was an excellent salesman but had a disdain for paperwork (as most good sales people do). This prevented him from getting promoted by his former employer into a managerial position, which, in turn, was lucky for me. The fact that he was not a good bureaucrat did not bother me. His sales ability was what counted. I simply put him in charge of an office manager who took care of the administrative details.

This brings up an important point. Most U.S. corporations over-emphasize administrative capabilities in their managers. For example, I know an air conditioner manufacturer* where the vice president of sales never sold an air conditioner; the vice president of technology never designed an air conditioner; the vice president of marketing sold farm machinery in his former job, and the vice president of manufacturing did not know the price of a pound of steel. Such management policies are a recipe for disaster!

The CEO has to rely on all these managers to make the decisions that affect the future of his or her company. In order to do this, each manager, in turn, has to rely on the knowledge and good will of his or her subordinates. Good will is especially important since if this particular manager is not well liked (quite common in this situation since a superior with a lack of technical knowledge is likely to develop an inferiority complex that manifests itself by rude behavior towards underlings), he will be mislead on purpose. The corporate staff, who may be well versed in preparing earnings forecasts, are much like a group of blind people trying to cross a busy street with the

---

* An assumed product to protect the innocent.

9

aid of guide dogs when it comes to deciding how to counter a competitive threat or how to pick a product that will keep the company from going under.

Leadership Qualifications

The moment you hire employees or you become a head of a department, you in effect become a leader. What kind of a leader do you want to be? Unquestionably, all of us want to be loved, respected, and admired. The reality is quite different. Your groups of employees or subordinates are quite a different bunch of people with diverse backgrounds and temperaments. Your carefully thought-out motivational strategy may work quite well with one or two persons, but may cause resentment or, worse, ridicule with others. This then calls for flexibility in your approach, and you have to take the time to study each person's personality. Never underestimate the intelligence of the people who work for you!

From my own, and admittedly very limited survey, here are the three most important characteristics that a boss should possess:

1. Honesty. This almost always comes first and covers such diverse matters as not being truthful about the financial conditions of the company, or pending layoffs (if you don't want to reveal such facts, say so, but don't fib), to promising raises or promotions, and then not following up and, even worse, stealing your subordinate's ideas.

10

2. Receptiveness. Be receptive to your employees' or subordinates' ideas or suggestions. This sometimes is hard to do since the idea may not always be practical or cost effective. Try to be open and make an honest effort to evaluate each case. If your decision is positive, then reward the person. If negative, take time from your busy schedule and explain the reasons.

3. Fairness. This covers a lot of ground and may quite often be perceived differently between several people. For example, a promotion is considered a fair and deserved action by the person receiving the promotion, but invariably may be resented as unfair by another employee. It extends to the way pay raises or work assignments are handed out, to how your bonus plan is structured.

One thing you should not forget in judging the attitude of your people is that at least 90% of them think they are perfectly qualified to take over your job and able to do it better than you. This leads us to what I consider a very important qualification of any boss: be capable of understanding and even performing any job or task that your subordinate is capable of doing. This way you can teach them to do their job better, and it will enable you to help them out if they run into difficulties.

If you can do this, you will earn their respect.... a much more valuable and effective trait over the long run than the elusive *being loved*.

The most important qualification you should have as an *effective* boss is to have a great memory. Let me explain. You have to be able to remember each suggestion or command you give during the day (probably to many people) and then check later to see if it has been done. The reason is simple. Many subordinates may not like your plan or command; therefore, they tend to *forget about it*. If you forget too, then they win the argument the quiet way. You lose, and nothing gets done. On the other hand, if you remember and bring the subject up again, they feel exposed and will think twice before trying to circumvent your orders again.

One thing you have to realize is that starting a company is lots of things, but most of all is extremely hard work. This requires stamina to work 60 hours plus a week and is not something you want to undertake if you are over 50 years old. You also have to be prepared to give up your hobbies, such as playing golf. And perhaps, worst of all, be prepared to spend less time with your family. All this has to be discussed thoroughly with your family prior to making this move. They are the ones who will suffer, at least during the first few years.

Of course, having a partner does help. First, you can split the initial investment and the high workload. Secondly, you have a confident (and not a disinterested employee) to share your problems and concerns with. It will help and be even better if the partner is your spouse or close friend and who has

12

suitable skills such as in accounting or personnel, for example. Handling the financial side is especially handy since this is an area where confidentiality and discretion are important.

However, before you start any undertaking with a partner, you better prepare an ironclad partnership agreement. A joint business venture is like a marriage; it can be a happy one and last forever, or it can end in a nasty divorce. You would be amazed to know how many taxi drivers I have met who claim they were cheated out of their businesses by a crooked partner. This brings up the next subject:

Legal Entanglements

I am not an attorney and having never been admitted to any bar, I should not tell you how to write agreements, even though you may be perfectly able and legally authorized to do so. Regardless of whether you or your attorney writes the contract, remember, the most important paragraph is the *escape clause*. In any good contract, there should be a specified way to terminate any contract without causing you or your partner irreparable harm. You should insist on this!

As long as there are attorneys, there will always be the chance that you may lose your business even without any fault of your own. You may be late with your loan payments, due to delays in customer payments, and the bank may want to repossess. Some disgruntled employee may sue you, or one of your products may have been installed in a factory that burned down and someone got hurt. The fact that your product had nothing to do with the fire is, unfortunately, no consideration when you are subpoenaed. It will cost you perhaps hundreds of thousands of dollars in legal fees to prove your innocence.

You may not have all that money to prove your innocence, especially when you are just starting out. You may also not have found an insurance company willing to write a product liability policy for an unknown company. So you may have to be prepared to fold your business before it really got started.

A friend of mine devised a special way to solve this dilemma. He arranged his company's finances in such a manner that the net assets were never more than a token sum. In other words, he withdrew any unneeded cash by paying dividends or distributions to his partners and then, in turn, put up outside loans (sometimes from the same partners) to balance whatever equity there was in business property or inventory. His thinking was that no attorney worth his salt would bother to sue a company whose net worth was zero. There wouldn't even be enough assets to pay his legal fees. I think my friend probably had something there.

How Much Starting Capital Do I Need?

The important thing is to keep your starting capital as low as possible. There are three reasons: (1) there is

14

less money to borrow or save, (2) with less capital invested, any profit will provide you with a higher rate of return on your capital, which looks good on your balance sheet and will impress future investors, and (3) with less capital there is less to lose should your new company become embroiled in a lawsuit.

Here are some ways to reduce capital needs:
(1) Lease buildings, automobiles, or even furniture.
(2) If you are a manufacturer, have your parts machined by a subcontractor.
(3) Subcontract at least a portion of your employees.

Now in order to estimate your starting capital requirements, first figure out your operating expense requirements for the first year. Table 1-1 may serve as a guide.

The data in this table are based on an assumed $1 million in sales per year. You may have to pro-rate the amounts shown in this table, i.e., use half the numbers if you shoot for only $500,000 in sales, or double the numbers for $2 million in yearly sales. Another thing I want to point out is that these figures are based on the assumption that you may want to start a manufacturing business and are somewhat on the lean side (i.e., you should be a good manager). For a wholesale business, the capital requirements are certainly less, but so will your profit level as a percent of sales.

15

Table 1-1
FIRST YEAR OPERATING EXPENSES
Based on $1 Million yearly Sales

	No Leases	Leased Equipment
Wages/salaries	$195,000	$195,000
Wage related overhead	57,000	57,000
Sales expenses	125,000	125,000
Advertising	10,000	10,000
Shipping expenses	20,000	20,000
Travel expenses	8,000	8,000
Telephone/fax	4,000	4,000
Insurance[*]	3,000	3,000
Supplies	5,000	5,000
Utilities	3,000	3,000
Legal/Accounting	5,000	5,000
Interest[**]	74,000	34,000
Cost of material	285,000	285,000
Rent/Lease payments	0	100,000
TOTAL	**$794,000**	**$854,000**
Profit before Tax and Depreciation: ($ 1 Mio Less Operating Expenses)	$206,000	$146,000
Return on Capital:	14%	21.5%
Profit as % of Sales:	20.6%	14.6%

---

[*] Could be substantially higher if product liability insurance is involved and you have no product history.

[**] Assuming a bank loan on 50% of starting capital (see Table 1-2) at 10% interest.

As you can see, it makes a difference on whether or not you lease buildings and tool machinery. If you own buildings and machinery, the yearly expenses are less $794,000 versus $854,000 when leasing due to the added lease payments. However, if you look at the capital requirements shown in Table 1-2, the situation is reversed. Without a lease, you need $1,475,000 and with a lease, you only need $680,000—or roughly half. Now the profit (before tax and depreciation) is $206,000 without a lease versus $146,000 with a lease. This makes a return on capital invested of 14.0% versus 21.5% before tax and makes leasing an attractive option, although you might miss the tax savings due to depreciation.

Notice that I added a ½-year's worth of expenses to the capital requirements. The fact that your initial sales will only start slowly and that customers typically pay their bills four to six weeks after the goods have been shipped to them, can make for a very tight cash situation at least for the first six months. This is a fact commonly overlooked by many budding entrepreneurs, who when faced by such an emergency have to go to such unpleasant means as delaying payment of salaries and taxes, or not paying their vendors. All actions fraught with great danger!

Table 1-2
REQUIRED STARTING CAPITAL
For projected sales of $1 Million per Year

	No Leases	Leased Equipment
Cash	$10,000	$10,000
Accounts receivable	115,000	115,000
Inventory	180,000	180,000
Deposits	5,000	25,000
Land	150,000	0
Building	200,000	0
Factory machinery	450,000	0
Small tools & fixtures	50,000	50,000
Vehicles	25,000	0
Computer software	5,000	5,000
Furniture/computers	25,000	5,000
Literature	5,000	5,000
6-month operating cash flow*	255,000	285,000
TOTAL	**$1,475,000**	**$680,000**

*50% of one-year operating expenses from Table 1-1 less cost of material (already included in inventory).

In some businesses, a reserve of half of the yearly expenses is not enough. For example, if you want to start out as a manufacturing representative in a new territory, then a year's expenses will be necessary as a safety cushion in order to keep you alive.

How to structure your company

Most people assume that the moment you start your own business you have to get incorporated. This is mostly unnecessary and quite often foolish. Let's review the advantages and disadvantages of the various options:

Proprietorship. This means you own your own business and there are no shareholders. The income passes directly to you and you report it on your IRS Form 1040, Schedule C. A big advantage is there are no paperwork hassles, franchise tax payments, and so on. The biggest disadvantage is that should you ever go bankrupt, your creditors will go after your private assets and bank accounts.

Incorporation (Inc.) Here your company becomes a separate legal entity with its own personality and rules. The corporation papers have to be filed with the Secretary of State, usually in the state where you live. The corporation has to follow certain specified rules such as having to have stockholder meetings, and elected officers. Tax disadvantages are that you have to pay double taxation unless your earnings are small, i.e., your corporation pays a corporate income tax, (IRS Form 1120) and your stockholders pay again a tax on dividends paid from the same earnings. For example, the maximum corporate tax rate for incomes above $325,000 at present (year 2000) is 39%. If you happened to be in the maximum tax bracket for your personal income which is 39.6 %, then you may wind up paying a total of 63% on your portion of the earnings of the corporation, quite a steep penalty. Note, the corporation has to pay taxes on income regardless whether it pays dividends or not.

Some people use a corporation to accumulate value by not paying dividends (you still have to pay corporate income taxes!). Later on, you can either sell the company (pay lower capital gain taxes), or leave the company to your children; however, there are better ways of doing this (read on). The biggest advantage of a corporation is that you can sell stock in the open market in order to raise cash for growth.

Also consider this; if you are a professional, such as an accountant or medical practitioner, your corporate umbrella does not protect you from professional liability (e.g., a malpractice suit).

A Limited Partnership (Ltd.). This means you must have at least one other partner. One of you has to be the "general partner," i.e., the person who runs the company and assumes all liability. "Limited partners," in contrast, are like stockholders; they are shielded from liability. On the other hand, limited partners are excluded from running the company, much like stockholders in a corporation. Since the general partner is liable for all debts, etc. it is prudent that the general partner should be a corporation in order to provide protection to the person who owns the general partnership. It is also possible to have a "Limited Liability Company" as a general partner (see below).

Other disadvantages include limitation in the number of partners and foreign ownership restrictions. Tax advantages include no double taxation, i.e., all earnings are taxed to you as an individual. A partnership files IRS form 1065. This is basically only an information return showing the IRS how much of the earnings are allocated to each partner.

No income tax is paid by the partnership itself except to some states in the form of business profit tax. Your personal tax liability for partnership profits can pose a cash flow problem, and the limited partnership usually has to pay at least sufficient funds to the partners enabling them to pay his or her income tax. This is cash not available for growth and expansion. Another limitation is that you cannot freely sell your share of the partnership, and you are typically required to obtain the approval of the other partners.

Limited Liability Companies (LLC). This is the latest, and only recently approved, form of business ownership. It basically combines most of the advantages of a corporation and those of a limited partnership. Hence, a "member" (that is part owner) of an LLC is shielded from liability (except criminal), and you do not need to have a general partner. There is also no limitation in the number of "members." The tax treatment is exactly like a partnership. To me, this is the best way to start your business. Perhaps the only drawback is the restriction of the transfer of shares. Nevertheless, you can always change the LLC into a corporation when your company has grown big enough to need lots of capital in order for you to become another Bill Gates. All owners or "members" theoretically can manage the company. Since this is sometimes impractical, you may want to elect a Management Committee, which can act in a similar way as a Board of Directors in a corporation.

Proprietorships, Ltd.'s, and LLC's all have one inconvenience. Apparently, the IRS does not trust these types of associations and all your customers, purchasing more than a few hundred dollars worth of product from your company, are required to file a form 1099 at the end of the year. This imposes a burden on them and, therefore, may hamper your sales efforts. The way out is to form a separate corporation that does only the selling and invoicing for the rest of the company, which then remains an LLC or Ltd., and, thus, avoids double taxation.

Do I need a Web Site?

Nowadays no respected businessman wants to be without a web site. With all the hype flying around, you have this vague feeling that no business can succeed without a Web site.

Let's look at reality, what can a web site accomplish?

First, there is simply *advertising*, i.e., customers look at your web site and find out where you are located, perhaps who your local representatives are, and what kind of products you produce or sell. This type of site is rather simple and you might even try to produce it

22

yourself (sites such as AOL even provide help for free). First, of course, you have to register a web site name, say JoeSmith.com, for example. This insures that you don't infringe on somebody else's name and that you have a unique I P address on the web. Simply contact *interNIC* (Phone 1-888-420-0063), among others, and pay a yearly fee of $35.

Before creating your web site, make a detailed plan of what information should be displayed. Picture yourself as a potential customer searching for a particular product. What questions might he or she have? Then provide the answers on your site. That may sound simple, but you would be surprised at the number of ill-designed sites on the Internet. Not long ago, I wanted to contact a large U.S. corporation with over $10 billion in sales. I went to their Internet site and found page after page of descriptions of their products, location of their divisions, how to make employment inquiries, and much more. However, among all the fluff there was neither a telephone number nor a street address listed that would enable an interested customer to contact the firm!

If you want to go into a *retail business* then things get dicey. You will definitely need professional help creating your web site, which has to be extremely user-friendly. Customers do not want to get frustrated when visiting your Web page.

Your site will not only need to display a description of your goods, with their respective price and order number, but you also have to provide means of money transfer (i.e., credit cards) with their respective security codes. Finally you have to arrange for shipping the goods to your customers. This can be a multi-million dollar task and a reason why most electronic vendors have not made profits in their venture.

Ask yourself this question: Why did Sears, one of the most successful catalog sales vendors, leave this business? If Sears could not sell enough with the aid of full-colored catalog pages on shiny paper, why do you think that a grainy, small picture on a monitor screen would sell more goods? Aside from the novelty, which will wear off, a web business is nothing but a mail-order business where the telephone is replaced by the keyboard.

So you have to sell products that are easy to identify in the minds of your potential customers. Books and musical recordings come to mind. All your customers have to do is read about a title in the newspaper and remember it. Besides, shipping costs are low and you do not have to worry about spoilage during transit as you might with groceries. Also, a good candidate is selling airline tickets. With other items, such as shoes or clothing, you should use caution. First, customers like to try the merchandise and feel the fabric, neither of which can be done over the Internet. And let's face it; the *Net* can never replace the atmosphere and human interaction that a shopping mall can provide.

Selling *manufactured goods* to other businesses electronically has already been done for about twenty

24

years. This includes electronic order transfer and electronic billing from the customer's computer to yours. While not Internet business, this was the closest thing yet. The problem with this system is that the program language of one customer differed from that of the next and none of these worked with your own system software. It was also quite expensive because it required dedicated computers and telephone lines. Here, the use of the Internet may help matters. The biggest problem again is proper software. While it is easy to order a book, which may simply be identified by a 6-digit number, for example, manufactured goods, especially those that are custom engineered to fit special customer requirements, may need very detailed text description. How about getting the customer's wishes and specifications via the Internet to you in the first place? All daunting questions for which there are no answers as yet. New technologies, such as XML, are on the horizon to help matters.

Ordering specialty items is, therefore, a much greater problem than the task of your purchasing department searching the Web for the price of a pound of gage 28 copper wire! In other words, *Internet trade lends itself more to commodities (grain, metals) and fairly common machine parts such as nuts and bolts than to complicated, mechanical or electronic devices!*

What you can do is try to design your products in such a way that they can fit into a great range of customer requirements and also meet both national and international standards and codes. The need for extensive descriptions and, most important, the need for a very elaborate selection process will thereby disappear. Your initial development process and manufacturing cost may be higher but will easily be offset by reduced overhead in your own order entry and planning departments, and by the reduction of inventory and higher sales volume.

How to find a financial angel

Besides investing the money from your savings or those of your friends', there is always the possibility to contact a venture capital outfit for additional capital.

These people are eager to invest in your company as long as there is the promise of a quick return in the form of profits. Your job is to convince them that this will happen, and fairly soon. It is not an easy task and one that requires great skill and planning on your part. To do this you need a BUSINESS PLAN.

Not long ago, all you had to do to get millions of dollars was to have a rudimentary web site and a company name ending with "dot-com." Alas, reality has set in since then and now you need to show something more substantial besides vague promises of future millions. That will take some work.

What you need first is a product or service for which there is *demonstrable demand.* Explain what is unique about it and makes it better than those of your competitors'. Also, get some outside opinion to your product idea *were* unique, then getting a patent or at least a patent application would be of help. Register at the Library of Congress as a trademark if you happen upon a catchy company name!

Study the market and tabulate your competitors' weak and strong points. The market research should include each competitor's market share and cost situation. Finally, determine ways to effectively distribute your products and services.

At this point, you reached a make or break point for your venture. Do not waste any more of your money or your time if the following cannot be proven:

1. There is at present no oversupply on the market for your products or services, and the market can absorb your future share.
2. Your competitors offer products or services that are inferior to yours, or ideally they don't have any.
3. You have a stronger cost basis than your competitors.
4. You have means to establish effective sales and distribution channels.

If you can honestly say "yes" to all of the above then continue.

The next step is to prepare the financial part of the Business Plan. This plan should extend at least over the next 5 years.

Starting with your anticipated sales forecast, prepare an *Operating Budget* for each year. Next draft the corresponding *Capital Budget* based on the capital requirements resulting from the operating budget. For more details on budgets consult Chapter 7.

If you are assuming that you will generate cash flow (and you better after the first year!), then any positive cash flow (profit plus depreciation) will lower your future capital demands. Allow for payback of loans and for payment of taxes!

Don't forget to add sufficient amounts for legal expenses in order to draw up a venture capital agreement and perhaps additional legal costs for S.E.C. filing fees, etc., if you want to "float" stock in your venture. This item alone will set you back several hundred thousands of dollars.

Put all of this into a neat binder and present it to your prospective venture capital provider such as the ones listed below.

Brighton Venture Partners, Softbank Venture Capital, Oak Investment Partners, VeriSign, Barksdale Group, Direct Equity Partners, Sequoia Capital, and Presidio Capital.

One final note, if your venture capital funding looks promising, then your financial angels most likely want to have the majority ownership of your business. Resisting this will put your personal salesmanship to the ultimate test.

Remember: *The outcome of any negotiation has nothing to do with fairness...only with skill!*

Finding the right location

As any good real estate agent can tell you, the most important factor determining the price of a house is its location. Any manager or entrepreneur likewise has to think very hard before deciding where to put his new division or new factory. The main considerations affecting such a decision are:

1. Availability of manpower.
2. Good infrastructure such as access to power, water, natural gas, and sewage facility.
3. A good road and transportation facility.
4. A favorable tax environment.
5. Availability and close access to sub-contractors and parts suppliers.
6. Possibility of obtaining State or municipality subsidized financing.
7. Attractive building sites.
8. Location near institutions of higher education and research facilities.

The order of importance may vary from case to case and there can be additional factors to consider.

Nevertheless, to evaluate everything takes a lot of time and energy. Then again, not doing a proper job can be very costly in the long run.

Sometimes, of course, there are other considerations such as in this case: The wife of a company chairman was unhappy because there was no opera house in the city where she was living. She, therefore, badgered her husband to relocate the corporate headquarters to a large metropolitan area.

This is a perfectly understandable step taken by her husband. After all what are a few million dollars of moving expenses compared to the possible lack of domestic bliss?

Next to obtaining low cost financing, perhaps by State guaranteed low cost loans, I would rate the tax consideration as most important, when it comes to selecting the State in which to locate your facility, and likely, your own residence. Here I would rate the absence of a State income tax of more importance than say the business profit tax. This is especially important if you want to be organized as a Limited Partnership or, a Limited Liability Company (see previous sub-chapter). The reason is simple, all business profit is considered personal income of the partners, or, the "members" of an LLC. Therefore, it is free from state taxes if you happen to live in a state with no personal income tax.

The following States have no personal income taxes (as of this writing): Texas, Tennessee, Nevada, Florida, Alaska, Wyoming, and New Hampshire. However, there may be other hidden taxes such as the Business Profit Tax, in New Hampshire.

30

Still this is not too bad since you can deduct most of the income as "personal services" by the partners and, therefore, still keep it State tax-exempt. Lest I be misquoted or misunderstood, please consult your tax advisor prior to making a final decision.

It is interesting to note that States with no income tax tend also to have the lowest amount of taxes per capita. Remember: *The difference between a highly taxed State and one with lower taxes per capita lies not in the level of services rendered to its citizens but in the number of State workers employed.*

As to the other issues, any State Economic Development Commission will be glad to supply you with information about their State, their work force, financial help, and other vital facts.

Chapter 2

How To Manage A Company, Or How Not To Follow The Old Rules

The purpose of a business is to make money,
not to make or sell widgets.

Having been employed for 23 years at small- and mid-sized corporations both in the United States and Europe, prior to forming my own company, allowed me the luxury of observing, firsthand, the many mistakes made by management. Mistakes that reduced profits and squandered valuable monetary resources. Perhaps even worse, bad decisions also can cause morale problems with the employees, most of whom are quite capable detecting and observing unsound decisions.

Why do many managers seemingly make irrational decisions? In my opinion, the reasons are in part because:

1. A manager was promoted to a position, which he is incapable of filling. This is the so-called *Peter's Principle* (from the book by Canadian educator Laurence J. Peter, published by William Morrow in *1969*).

2. Frequently managers do not understand basic business principles on how to generate profit. In other words, they are not trained to think like entrepreneurs.

3. Related to the above, most managers, even CEOs that have progressed through lower positions maintain a tendency to adhere to unwritten company rules (don't *rock the boat!*).

4. Managers are very security conscious. Unfortunately, not conscious of their company's security, but of their own. This stifles initiative.

5. Often managers and CEOs blindly follow the latest trend or fad in their given field of business. It may be ISO 9000, or the latest software packages, without regard to cost-benefits. (However, that way they appear to be modern in the eyes of their peers!).

6. Many managers are incapable of understanding technical or intricate financial problems in their department and, therefore, have to rely on the advice of their staff. This can lead to *blind* decision-making. The manager may have been promoted into his or her position through *seniority* or *connections* rather than expertise in a given field.

33

Besides the apparent ineptitude of some of my former managers, I also learned that many unsound company decisions were based on bad marketing, or worse, to satisfy some obscure internal financial habits.

A case in point: A mid-size corporation I worked for some years ago purchased a smaller valve manufacturing company founded twenty years earlier by a clever engineer and entrepreneur. In order to reduce his initial capital investment, he decided to forego the purchase of expensive machine tools and instead subcontracted the machining of all parts. This left, besides administrative personnel, only a few assembly workers. The results were a consistent 25% to 28% profit before tax--a fact that made the takeover attractive to an outside buyer (my employer) when the owner decided to retire.

After the formal takeover of this well-run company by my employer, the accountants of my company were in for a shock. They were used to allocating certain overhead expenses onto the hourly wages of the shop employees. In this case there were not enough i.e. there were not enough direct hours to absorb the overhead burden! Distributing all the overhead expenses on the few workers available would have looked ridiculous on the balance sheet. In other words, the Accounting Department of the purchasing company was unable to do proper cost accounting under their own well-established rules for the products made by the acquired firm.

This situation created quite a panic within top management. After some frantic meetings, it was decided, rather than accept the otherwise quite logical situation, to instead purchase machine tools for several million dollars and hire the requisite number of machinists (more *direct* labor). This satisfied the accountants, but caused havoc with the efficiency of this smaller, purchased plant. Its profits dropped by 60% within the first year after being purchased!

I never forgot this valuable lesson, and my first action after forming my own firm was to find outside vendors to do the machining of my parts. *This should be Rule No. 1!* Besides the obvious savings in capital and floor space, there are other not so obvious advantages. One is the saving in labor with the associated headaches of personnel problems, training, pensions, etc. Another advantage of great importance is the absolute predictability of product cost. The total cost of a finished item is simply the sum of the listed invoiced amounts for the individual parts. You simply don't pay the invoice if a part is machined wrong (formerly you had to absorb the cost as overhead in your own machine shop). Incidentally, this works wonders for your Quality Control Department too.

Aside from assembly time, which is pretty constant, there are very few variable cost items, which make it possible to have a very accurate profit and cost statement at the end of each month.

Rule No. 2 is to try to avoid having a Human Resource or Payroll Dept. Related to the above is the effort to have as few employees as possible. (This includes part-time or out-sourced employees--a ruse used by many managers to by-pass strict, no-hire policies!) The result, besides the obvious increase in profit, is no need for a Human Resource and Payroll Department, at least for companies with fewer than 100 employees. All payroll work can be out-sourced to data processing companies who, for a few dollars per employee, can also keep track of the never-ending Federal and State rules and regulations besides filing timely payroll tax returns for your company. Screening new employees can be done by employment agencies. I encourage you to hire temporary help as long as you don't do it to pull the wool over your bosses eyes by pretending you have less workers on the payroll than there are actually working, i.e., showing a low payroll on your monthly profit and loss report. If they work out, then you can always hire them later. If they don't fit, then all it takes is a phone call to terminate their employment without any messy legal entanglements.

Rule No. 3 is do not use a Purchasing Department. The next *not to have* on my list is a Purchasing Department. While still young, I observed that a purchasing agent seldom knows the ins and outs of what to purchase. He or she relies instead on written requisitions from other departments who specify quantity and, usually, vendor sources. This convinced me that the job of typically re-typing a pre-written requisition from say the planning department on to a purchase order form is a very non-essential activity.

So instead of a person in the factory writing a requisition for a given material, he or she simply generates the purchase order himself. This not only saves personnel, but also time (delivery time is the key to a customer's happiness). Well, you may ask, how about the skill of a good purchasing agent to negotiate prices, or to avoid conflict of interest or bribes? These are mostly myths. I cannot recall having met a Purchasing Manager who understood the technical requirements, the quality aspects, and delivery needs, as well as the person who needs the part of the equipment. Besides, the initial vendor selection should always be based on multiple price quotation. Otherwise, the up to 20% margin on top of the parts prices to cover the cost of a Purchasing Department saved makes up for some improprieties (should it happen).

Rule No. 4 is don't split lines of responsibility. What I mean by that is to make sure that a single manager, who assumes full responsibility, controls vital functions. For example, if you have a Plant Manager who is responsible for producing and shipping out goods to your customers on time, make sure he has complete control of procurement for parts and material. If you don't, then you have to listen to endless complaints and excuses why an order was delayed. The Production Manager will blame the Purchasing or Planning Manager for not getting material or parts, and the latter will complain for not getting a timely requisition or sales forecast. You will begin to pull your hair out!

Another obsession with efficiency of modern management is inventory turn over (ITO). This is driven by financial consideration.... a low inventory means more cash is available for investment. This sounds good in theory, but not always a profitable way to do business.

In my company, the turnover ratio was a measly 2.5; that is, a given part stayed on the shelf for about five months. This is, of course, an average figure. Some parts stayed less than three months, others for eight or nine months. The reasons were two-fold: First, instead of buying smaller quantities of goods many times, we purchased larger quantities typically four times a year. This gave us substantially lower costs from our vendors (less set up time). Secondly, by keeping a *high* inventory, we virtually never ran out of parts. What this meant was that we could fulfill 90% plus of all customers orders in a matter of hours and at a hefty premium!

Here is a little math to show you how this "disrespect" for ITO paid off. Assume you have a $10 million inventory when the ITO is 2.5, and an inventory of $6.25 million with an ITO of 4. The extra capital outlay to carry the inventory for 4.8 months (ITO = 2.5) instead of the desired 3 months (ITO = 4) at say 9% bank interest is:

$$(\$10,000,000 - \$6,250,000) \times .09$$
or $337,500 per year.

Suppose with an inventory turnover of 2.5 ($10 million in stock) we can ship 10% of all goods on an expedited delivery schedule (because we have parts on hand) and assuming further that the average sales price is 2.6 times inventory cost. The extra profit earned based on a 15% *quick ship* add on is:

$$0.10 \times 2.5 \times 2.6 \times \$10,000,000 \times 0.15$$
$$\text{or } \$975,000 \text{ per year.}$$

That is a 260% return on money *wasted* in inventory! To that, you have to add up to $6.5 million of extra sales volume because your competitors cannot match your delivery schedule. One has to realize that this inventory leverage disappears quickly with a decrease in gross profit. For example, if the gross profit had only been 35% instead of the assumed 61.5%, then the return on quick ship sales would have only been $576,932 instead of $975,000.

Since my former companies gross profit averaged 68%, i.e., the inventory (cost of parts) was only 32% of the average sales price, we effectively turned the inventory over an impressive 7.8 times when compared to the sales volume (yearly sales volume divided by the value of inventory). This compares to only about 6 times inventory on sales volume by my larger competitors. Let's call this *Rule No. 5*.

It turned out that I was not alone in this philosophy. The former New Hampshire based Cabletron Corporation with over $1 billion in yearly sales prior to the departure of their owners/founders had an ITO of less than 3 but a turnover of sales to inventory of close to 8:1! Need I say that Cabletron had profits of about 35% before tax? Not surprisingly, their business philosophy was identical to my own. Keep as much inventory on hand to sell every product off-the-shelf. It was the key to their phenomenal growth rate compared to their competitors who followed rigid accounting rules.

Rule No. 6 concerns how you train your employees. As rightly pointed out by Hammer and Champy[*] modern workers, especially in non-factory occupations, should be trained to be *generalists* instead of *specialists*; that is, employees should be trained to perform several tasks. This, almost by default, requires they be given freedom to make decisions. It is probably less harmful for a company to allow employees to make occasional mistakes than to establish a too rigid hierarchical management system.

A case in point: Internal sales people in my former company performed multiple functions starting with such mundane tasks as answering the telephone and entering customer orders into the computer to advising customers on technical problems (with backup from engineering if required), to selling to customers and writing million-dollar quotations. That was all done in a day's work and it created not only a

---

[*] Hammer and Champy, *Reengineering the Corporation,* (New York: Harper Business, 1993)

lively workday (no boredom here), but also a spirit of camaraderie.

In another company I happened to know quite well, the sales department was rigidly departmentalized. First, the telephone is routed through an operator and through the infamous *voice mail*. Second, the sales people were forbidden to talk directly to customers (all customer requests were to be referred to the local sales representative). Third, there was to be no more direct sales effort by company people. Fourth, all internal sales staff was subdivided into geographical areas of responsibility, each handling only an assigned number of representative firms. The invariable result was that employee *A* had his or her phone mail overloaded while employee *B* in the *cubicle* next to him or her (yes, everybody had the cubicle space made famous by the *Dilbert* cartoon character!) went for a walk through the shop out of sheer boredom.

Rule No. 7 is don't use organizational charts. This sounds like a strange request, but it need not be. Along with titles, organization charts tend to *lock* managers into specific duties rather than utilizing their talents over as wide a spectrum as possible. Don't worry, an employee will always know who his or her boss is even without a title or slot on the organization chart. I ran my multi-million dollar company for 18 years without ever needing a chart. But I had to invent one in a hurry to satisfy the buyer of my company during due diligence.

Rule No 8. Do away with headquarters staff. Larger corporations should do away with their headquarters staff departments such as Legal, Finance, Environmental, Human Resources, etc. Those are like a cancerous growth in an organism. Not only do they have to be paid for by *allocations of corporate expenses* to be paid for by individual divisions, but they, like government bureaucracy, want to extend their power and influence by telling you how to organize your cost system, how to interview personnel, send you endless safety advice, and so on. All this is done with the very best of intentions. The trouble is certain rules that may apply to an 800,000 square foot plant may not apply to one at 30,000 square feet. This *benevolent burden* hits especially smaller subsidiaries or plants. An *Environmental Manager* in a larger plant has time to interact with the respective corporate vice president and his or her staff, but with a smaller plant, the burden falls perhaps on the Plant Manager who is kept from making sure the shipping schedule is met for the month. Instead, he is commanded to an urgent meeting 1,000 miles away to discuss the impact of the latest Federal Regulations.

Mr. Koch, President of the Koch Company, one of the largest privately held U.S. corporations, has the right idea. Let your corporate staff compete on the open market. Instead of simply imposing a forced fee (allocations) onto your division, let each division contact a local attorney (if, for example, there is a legal problem) and the corporate legal staff. Find out which is less expensive and proceed accordingly. Mr.

Koch apparently knows what he is doing. Too bad he does not publish his profit statements. I suspect it is quite good.

Rule No. 9 is try to avoid fads. Falling for popular fads is quite easy. The peer pressure is great, the media bombards you (especially when it comes to Internet matters), and your sales manager will tell you the particular fad is one of *absolute necessity,* and your company will fail if you don't oblige and spend hundred thousands of dollars on a project that has no *demonstrable* impact on either sales or profit. Resist the trend even if it makes you seem old fashion in the eyes of your managers. Wait and see if the trend prevails and, most of all, if it helps your bottom line. The fact that your competitors do it should be the *least of reasons* to follow suit!

A case in point: About 10 years ago, The International Standards Organization came out with something called ISO 9000. It almost instantly developed into a fad and no manufacturer worth his salt would be without it even though it was very expensive to get approval from the certifying agency. You had to have consultants, revamp your operating procedures, etc. Besides you had to be reviewed every year in order to keep your certificate current. Despite urgings and dire warnings of my sales manager that non-certification would mean the loss of major customers. I resisted probably being the only manufacturer in my field to be non-certified. Guess what, we did not lose one single order, and I saved the company a bundle of money. Well, you might argue,

43

is it not a good idea to have all your systems and workflow recorded in writing (the premise of ISO 9000)? Probably! However, you can do this yourself and at your leisure. Most people don't realize it but you can be "self-certified," thereby saving all the money for outside consultants.

Another "must" is to have a *web site*. This may have some advertising value, but don't expect people to go to your web site and order industrial equipment from you and pay with a credit card. This is wishful thinking, and you should recognize it.

One of the current "Fads" is training sessions for employees that teach them how to get along with each other and to dress properly (not an easy task—"What is a proper informal dress code?"). While this may be time consuming, typically four sessions at four hours each and, therefore, eating into the company's profits, it may be justified to a minor extent to preempt future lawsuits by disgruntled employees.

Of a more serious nature is the latest trend to make employees laugh. The minimum recommendation is 20 minutes a day. Humor consultant Marianne Nunes, for example, encourages pillow fights. Others encourage slapstick behavior at the workplace and that at up to $1,000 per hour consulting fees.

Never mind that all this costs money (i.e., profit) and valuable company time, but what may be worse is that a company manual advocating these things looks ridiculous and immature in the eyes of most employees leading to a credibility crisis when it comes to making sound business decisions.

For following the above rules, you and your company may be rewarded with something resembling the following financial results, which reflect my own company's balance sheet the year prior to the sales of its assets:

Yearly sales volume per company employee:[*]	$364,000
Net profit before taxes as percent of sales:	32%
Yearly return on original capital invested before tax:	290%
Yearly return on working capital before tax:	52%

And remember, "Profit is the only form of praise for a job well done which cannot be bought."

Rule No 10. Dispense with Performance Reviews, or Performance Appraisals. While supposedly serving a good purpose i.e. keeping the employee abreast of his progress in the firm and to inform him how he performs his job assignments, at least in the eyes of his immediate supervisor, it has a number of drawbacks. First such reviews can be biased, i.e. they can reflect the personal feelings between the employee and his boss. We all have our personal biases or likes and dislikes. An up-grade or a downgrade based on our (sometimes sub-conscious) feelings is difficult to avoid.

---

[*] Price adjusted for the year 2000. Incidentally, I consider this figure my most important management tool even though hardly anybody else seems to think of it.

Secondly, most supervisors are not trained properly to conduct a meaningful review. The result is a patchwork of paper entries designed more to complete the form (duplicating essentially all of last years entries) in order to meet the minimum requirements of the human relation department, and, most important not to hurt the employees' feelings with a bad review. To avoid the latter, bosses tend to give only positive reviews. This results in "grade inflation" and fosters unrealistic wage and advancement expectations in the employee. An honest job appraisal results typically in a disappointment of the employee while a dishonest one maintains the status quo, even though it serves no purpose!

Another major drawback of an inflated job review is that it can backfire on the employer upon the job termination of an individual. He may then sue his company for wrongful dismissal. What do you think a jury will decide when it sees that this individual got only "good" and "excellent" marks in his yearly performance reviews? You guessed it "discrimination" is proven!

It is therefore better to dispense with the whole charade. Replace it with periodic and informal discussions between worker and supervisor. Make sure, every employee can have ready access to a higher level of management in case of grievances, or cronyism by the immediate boss.

Rule No 11. Don't move any capital-intensive operations abroad. When companies grow there is a tendency to open up subsidiaries abroad. This is partly done to be closer to the local markets for faster delivery and responsiveness to local requirement, or, in case of less developed countries to relocate manufacturing operations over-seas in order to take advantage of low cost wages. The first reason, relocate for marketing reason can make sense. You may want to have a local office in a particular country and even add to that an assembly and a service facility. However, do this only after you find a competent *local* general manager and after you did a thorough market analysis! The most common mistake is to take a US manager and transplant him abroad. The second biggest mistake is to neglect local prejudices and cultural languages. For example never use an Englishman to run a French subsidiary! This is a quite common mistake since you feel more comfortable with the British; after all, they all speak the same language. Resist this temptation, language will turn out to be the least of your worries.

As to manufacturing subsidiaries, stay away from any planned facility that requires major capital investments such as modern machine tools. As described later in another chapter, the apparent cost savings are nil compared to the overhead, capital depreciation and training costs. Just to compare wages while neglecting capital costs is the height of follies. However, there are ways to take advantage of low wages. This is in assembly operations. Take electronic components for example where hand assembly, or

47

hand soldering is required. Here, you need little capital except for a building, hand tools and some benches. Training is minimal and the only other cost considerations are local taxes and shipping expenses.

These are simple, but very often neglected rules. As the October 9, 2000 issue of *Business Week* stated under "Economic Trends": Corporate America poured $ 273 billion into foreign investments between 1998 and 1999 alone, yet the stock market value of companies that invested heavily abroad was between 9% and 17% lower than other firms without such investments. This is a sobering fact and an indication that most firms that invest abroad do a poor job of planning and execution. The subsequent losses, or low profit return from their foreign investments in turn depressed their market value.

One final bit of advice. No matter how much you are tempted, try not to be the first to buy a new device, equipment, or tooling even if it is highly recommended. The reason is simple…. any new technology needs time to mature, i.e., to eliminate the initial design defects and other shortcomings. In addition, first production runs tend to be rather expensive (the initial tooling and R&D expenses have to be absorbed). Therefore, the wise counsel is to be patient and wait until your competitors have tried it. While competitors may get more advertising mileage for being *technically up-to-date*, (or for being cool), they are also saddled with training their employees, higher maintenance expenses, unexpected breakdowns, and other unpleasantness directly affecting their bottom line.

A case in point is numerically controlled machine tools. When they came on the scene in about 1972, they were of limited use, had primitive electronics prone to breakdowns, and were hard to program. Yet, few manufacturers wanted to be left out of having at least one, lest they be accused of being old-fashioned.

When one of my friends (the president of a larger manufacturing firm) asked me what he should do, I counseled patience. Sure enough, within four to five years numerically controlled machine tools became a well working and, today, an indispensable tool of modern production. By waiting, my friend bought himself well-working products while saving himself all the expensive headaches of the earlier users.

Chapter 3

Rules For Successful Management

1. Manage your business to make profit first and then manufacture or sell widgets.

2. Try to have only four layers of management in each plant or division.

3. Become, and stay, the master of your computer systems.

4. Design your computer software program to enter, produce, and ship customer orders, and *not* to satisfy the Accounting Department.

5. Don't do or buy things because they are nice or fashionable. Purchase only what is absolutely necessary! This is especially true for your computer/information system where the *Fad de Jour* can be extremely expensive.

6. Solve problems immediately. They cost you twice as much after one-week and four times as much after one month, at which time you've lost a customer.

7. Do not manage by committee. Most successful managers are benevolent dictators.

8. Keep your lines of communication short and avoid meetings like the plague.

9. The most efficient company is a small company (see *Law of the Sphere*). If you have to grow, then subdivide.

10. Do not ask your subordinates to do things you would not be able or willing to do yourself. *

11. A well-run department can do all the required work within eight hours a day!

---

* While most of the above rules should be self-explanatory, I feel the need to elaborate why you, the boss, should be able to do the work performed by your subordinates. First, it is a good morale builder knowing that you are more than a remote person in the office. Secondly, if there is a problem, say with lack of parts, or machining tolerances, the worker knows that you can understand the problem at hand, and, therefore are able to speedily resolve it. Thirdly, by observing the workflow, you can see areas of improvement. The underlings will be more comfortable in asking questions regarding their work. Finally, by casually glancing over their shoulders you may spot errors or mishandling that the person is not even aware of. This gives you the chance to gently rectify the errors through teaching by example.

12. Do not create departments whose work can be done elsewhere, and assign managers to non-profit contributing departments on a temporary basis only.

13. Don't fall for fads such as ISO 9000. They can be very expensive. (However, encourage your competitors to do so!). This is not to say that you should omit having written records for all *major* tasks such as an order entry procedure, for example.

14. If there are any questions left, use your common sense first before going to outside consultants

15. Train your managers so they are able to run their departments without any external guidance, including your own.

16. Have a *real* person greet your customers when they call your company and outlaw all voice mail (except, perhaps, for interoffice use).

17. Follow up on a given assignment after about one week time, this will assure that the task it not forgotten by an employee who may not like to do it. A follow-up will convince him you mean business. No follow-up will tell him or her that you forgot about the assignment, a clear sign that you can be ignored in the future too.

Chapter 4

Incentives and Disincentives

Money outweighs coercion
when it comes to work incentives

As Scott Adams[*] (a.k.a. Dilbert) rightfully pointed out, "Nobody likes to work, otherwise people would pay their employers for the privilege."

What we need are incentives to cause otherwise healthy and smart people to get off their couches or leave the golf courses to go to a factory or office. Compensation, of course, is a powerful incentive. We all require money to pay for the necessities of life such as food, clothing, rent, or even alimony payments. But salary or wages alone are not often enough to stimulate a cohesive workforce, unless the pay is related directly to a measurable performance such as payment for the number of widgets produced

---

[*] Scott Adams, "The Dilbert Principle," (Harper Collins, 1996).

in an hour or a commission on a sale. Unfortunately, the output of the overwhelming majority of the labor force cannot be directly measured so it behooves management to provide incentives to encourage labor to work *voluntarily* towards a common goal, such as a company's profits.

In order for incentives to be effective, they must be (a) measurable, (b) guaranteed, (c) fair, (d) time limited, and (e) stimulate group performance. Incentive plans that do not meet these requirements are a waste of money, time, and effort. Governments try to stimulate employee group performance in state-run enterprises by appealing to ideology, patriotism, and by telling employees they are working for their own company (since the government is run by the people and the factory is run by the government; hence, the factory is owned by the people!). None of this works as the politicians of the former Soviet Union found out to their chagrin.

After starting my own company, I thought an incentive plan would help motivate my employees. Besides, I truly wanted my employees to feel that they were a part of the enterprise. While I maintained a separate bonus plan for key managers to stimulate specific tasks such as increasing sales, I devised a very simple plan to distribute a portion of the company's profits to all other employees. Since the company was on a fiscal calendar year, we would pay about 1/2 of the estimated bonus before Christmas and the final balance (after the books were audited) around the middle of March. The percentage was based on half of the net operating profit before interest and tax and usually amounted to between 9.5% and 12.8% of an employee's yearly wages or salary.

Having two payouts is psychologically important. Like any pleasurable experience in life, the biggest and longest lasting effect lies in *expecting* the benefits. We derive as much, if not more, pleasure *looking forward* to taking a vacation than actually experiencing the trip itself, which may turn out to be disappointing depending upon the circumstances. This is even truer when paying a bonus. The pleasure of expecting the money increases in inverse proportion to the waiting period for the money. Once the money is deposited, the bonus becomes a past event and its value to the employee quickly diminishes. Therefore, having two pay periods increases the stimulus. Any payout period exceeding one year becomes too long for proper stimulation. The brain cannot comprehend time periods of several years.

It is also important to keep the employees informed periodically about the estimated profits of the company. This will keep up the reward expectancy. As for fairness, it goes without saying that management should never renege on awarding bonuses, nor change the terms *during* a business year. One of the most important, beneficial effects of a group incentive is to stimulate the performance of the whole company. Here is where a good profit sharing plan shines. Every employee knows without prompting (sometimes by hideous cartoon-type posters put up by management) that company profits depend not only on his or her own performance, but also on the performance of their fellow workers. I have had employees go to their supervisors to complain about certain individuals who *were not performing well* and recommended they be reprimanded! It also prompts other company beneficial actions such as employees notifying supervisors of low inventory on certain key parts, volunteering overtime in order to ship an emergency order to a customer, and so on. What is most important is that this striving for effectiveness as an organization extends beyond the individual's department. It was not uncommon for an individual to volunteer to help out in another department busier than his own. All traits absent in companies having only individual performance-based bonuses, or none at all!

As an example, I know of a company that was sold to a much larger organization (with the group bonus plan still intact). The new president, doing what was customary in his former place of work, called an *all employees* group meeting which consisted of a pep talk outlining the future of the company in such terms as *S.I.P., ITO, best cost producer, order fulfillment, customer satisfaction actions, product differentiation, enterprise system,* and other terminology and acronyms which were new and incomprehensible to the bewildered employees who were accustomed to being addressed in plain English by the former CEO. The rest of the day was spent watching safety-related videos made by some *not-for-profit* department of the parent corporation (after purchasing a theater size video screen and matching high-power amplifying system) to teach how not to step in front of a forklift or how to recognize the color code of dangerous chemical containers (never used in this company).

The next day I talked with one of the employees who looked gloomy. She responded to my query on how the meeting went by saying: "Well, it was okay, but we lost a full day of production. I wonder how it will affect our profit-sharing bonus?"

As I previously stated, individual performance bonuses are okay, but only for managers of key departments. Even here, discretion and strategic planning are important. For example, it is a common temptation to give the sales manager a bonus tied to the order volume of a company. This is a serious error that will result in an instant increase in the discount given to customers with a resultant decrease in the profit level of the company. The sales manager knows quite well that if you extend the discount level over that of your competitors, you book more orders; hence, a bigger bonus.

However, the larger discount comes straight off the bottom line, i.e., the company profit. So, while you are able to sell more widgets, you wind up selling them at a lower profit or, worse yet, at a loss. In effect, by giving a bigger bonus to your sales manager, you reward him for the company's loss of profit!

I overcame this problem by making the sales bonus tie into the profit figures. For example, if bookings went up 5 percent over the prior year, and the profit was 20 percent, then his total bonus was $5 \times 20/10 = 10$ percent of his annual salary. However, if bookings went up 20 percent over the target set at the beginning of the year (and agreed upon by the manager), and the profit was only 2 percent, then his bonus was reduced to $20 \times 2/10 = 4$ percent! Thus, by discounting too much and, therefore, reducing the company's profit, his bonus got cut by 60 percent. This is a powerful incentive not to decrease prices unnecessarily.

A similar bonus plan can be devised for a production manager. Here the key next to profit could be *ship-on-time*. For instance, a bonus plan could look like this: Bonus = % profit $\times$ (% ship-on-time^2/10,000). If profit is 12% and ship-on-time is 78%, then the bonus is $12 \times (78^2/10,000) = 7.3\%$. If ship-on-time is 98% (as it should be!), then the bonus is 11.5%. This is a powerful incentive to service the customer.

In his book, *Reengineering Management*,[*] James Champy quoted Ira Walters of AT&T Universal Card Services: "The essence of our compensation program is divided into two components. One is our base pay, which is fairly typical. Then we have a rather rich variable pay program which is contingent on business outcomes thus supporting a company-wide incentive plan." A similar plan by Hannaford Bros. Company

---

[*] James Champy, *Reengineering Management,* (London, United Kingdom: Harper Collins, 1995)

was also quoted as being based on overall company budget achievement. In this case, the yearly bonus averaged about 9%. No wonders both of these companies are successful.

Regardless of the bonus, I made it a point to remind my managers several times during the year that *the company is in business to make money (profit), NOT to manufacture and sell widgets.*

While this message may seem hostile to the needs of customers, it really is not. Only a healthy and profitable company is of any use to a customer. This really touches on the heart of the private enterprise system and is what ultimately distinguishes us from socialistic economies. It is therefore paramount for a company president to remind managers of this simple message.

As I mentioned before, putting a whole group on individual performance bonuses will kill the cohesiveness and teamwork of the organization and, therefore, is counter-productive. For example, to make the bonus of a factory worker dependent on the sales increase is useless. So is the dependency of the bonus of sales associates on the quality level of the factory. This will cause resentment since neither is able to influence such a bonus requirement.

Other disincentives are perpetuating the purpose of a department whose function, while necessary, is basically profit reducing. Departments dealing with environmental issues come to mind. How can you motivate a manager of such a department to do his best to solve a particular plant clean-up problem and to deal effectively with the involved government agency? The manager knows quite well that with the resolution of this problem, his job may be terminated. The incentive is to *drag* the problem out. To help solve this problem, make this position a temporary transfer from another (profit contributing) department. I am sure this person would be itching to get back to his old job as soon as possible.

A prime example of this type of *absolute* disincentive can be found in the Federal Government. Take the National Cancer Institute, for example. The purpose of the institute is to search for a cure for cancer. Why then does it seem this institute does hardly anything more than design posters to encourage us to stop smoking? The answer should be obvious. Once there is a cure, then there is no more need for this institute. This is the ultimate disincentive.

Picture yourself as the head of the National Cancer Institute with over 5,000 employees, a *zillion* dollar budget*, etc. Suddenly a young scientist enters your office and excitedly proclaims, "Sir, I found a cure for cancer!" You would be sorely tempted to shoot the fellow on the spot for threatening your job security.

---

* During 1994, the U.S. Government spent $15,900 million on medical research (Source: *Statistical Abstract of the United States* (Government Printing Office, 1996)

Here is a summary of incentives and disincentives:

GOOD	**BAD**
Group incentives (profit sharing)	No incentive
Managerial performance tied to profit and performance	Individual incentives
Make non-profit contributing jobs distasteful.	Managerial incentives tied to functional performances only.
Make every employee feel he or she is part of a *family*.	Make non-profitable jobs a career position.

Chapter 5

Entropy and Other Heady Stuff

*A person avoiding work is but following
his or her instinct to conserve energy.*

In order to explain some basic human behavior such
as spending money rather than earning it, sitting in
committee meetings rather than doing actual work, or
enjoying skiing downhill but loathe walking up the
hill, we have to consult the laws of nature, or more
precisely, the laws of thermodynamics.

Thermodynamics, which to most is an obscure
scientific term, governs our daily lives whether we
realize it or not. Like other scientific disciplines,
fundamental laws govern it: Law number one
basically states, *no energy is ever lost*. Law number
two states that *energy always degrades to a lower
state*, which means it becomes less usable.

While the first law of thermodynamics gives false hopes of never-ending energy sources, thus encouraging unlimited use of available energy (or tax dollars as the economic equivalent), it is the second law's effect we feel. It manifests itself in such things as the continuing decrease in the average American's standard of living since about 1980[*] due in part to an ever-higher tax burden. This trend finally got reversed in the late 1990's due to the great strides in our economy with the result that the increase in Gross National Product exceeded tax payments. This in turn reduced the National Debt and increased living standards.

In scientific terms, when energy *decays* to a lower level, its *entropy* changes, i.e., there are fewer degrees per BTU (or degrees per calorie) than before. A similar example in economic terms is inflation. Here the change in entropy is equivalent to more dollar bills for the same loaf of bread. We obey this fundamental law at a very young age. Babies enjoy dropping their toys to the floor (expending energy to a lower level from crib to floor), while parents pick up the toy (this increases the available energy by bringing the toy up from the floor). We all recall the expression of satisfaction on the baby's face followed by the frown of the parent. Obviously, the baby is having much more fun.

---

[*] *Statistical Abstract of the United States*, Bureau of Census (median income of families, wife not in paid labor force, in constant 1994 dollars)

While steam is the classic carrier of energy in a process plant and loses pressure after passing through a steam engine, thereby *losing available energy* (entropy changes per the second law), so does the value of money if more is spent than available through the production of goods. Note, that I only said through goods not services. While only a good fire under a steam boiler can restore the original steam pressure (thus restoring the original entropy), basically only productive activities in areas such as farming, mining, and manufacturing can restore the value of money, i.e., increase its available energy (entropy) level.

It should be realized that like steam, money is essentially a carrier of energy for our economic system. It would not be far-fetched to peg the value of the dollar on a given number of calories instead of to the weight of gold as has been done before. A number of dollars per barrel of oil could be the measure of international currency, for example.

To make the concept of entropy more understandable, let's consider an example. You are faced with a rock located on top of a hill and one below. To roll the rock down takes very little effort. What we are doing is reducing the available energy (height of the hill times the weight of the rock) to a lower level. On the other hand, lugging the rock uphill is a lot of work and it takes toil and sweat.

This example illustrates how easy it is to expend energy, i.e., spend money rather than make it. In political terms, it takes hardly any effort for a

64

Congressman to vote for a measure that increases expenditure than to vote for a measure that reduces spending. Subconsciously he abides by the second law of thermodynamics. We experience the same in our personal lives. How easy it is to spend a dollar; how hard it becomes to earn it!

With few exceptions, all services performed reduce the available energy of our monetary system. It is, therefore, not possible, as many fashionable book authors have predicted in the 1980s, that the entire United States would convert from a primarily industry-based economy to that of a service-based economy where we all sit at home and work on computers. The result would be a rapid decrease in value of our money since there will no longer an *increase in available energy* (increase in monetary value) due to manufacturing.

Most politicians have a legal background and their exposure to science, let alone thermodynamics, is limited. How else can one explain their decision to build windmills, which during their lifetime of perhaps 20 years, produce significantly less power than is consumed in the process of melting the steel, copper, and in the machining of parts, in order to produce these windmills. This exercise in futility under the noble name of using *free energy*, i.e., the wind, is only possible by masking the basic economic facts with taxpayer money, i.e., cover the production energy deficit with monetary energy (Government grants and tax credits)[*]. If wind power were really cheap as claimed, you would have seen electric companies exploiting this source years ago! It should also be noted that government forces conventional power plants to buy the electric output of so-called *renewable energy sources* at a cost per kW hour substantially above their own cost. Guess who pays for the difference...the consumer.   This again is a classic example of the second law of thermodynamics in action! Available energy (national wealth) is reduced to a lower usable level (uneconomical windmills!). It may not be a bad idea to give each politician a crash course in the economics of energy. Our country would certainly be better off.

In terms of management policy, consider all administrative or supportive functions as *changing the energy* (of your company) to a lower level. Money (like energy) is spent in the form of salaries, while no profit (excess energy) is generated.   Effective personnel involved directly in the production of goods do increase energy, and, therefore, does generate profit (it increases the available energy in the form of monetary value).

---

[*] *DER SPIEGEL*, Vol. 32, (Augstein VVerlag: Germany, 1990), p. 91.

Chapter 6

Meetings, or Managing
   By Committee

*Committee decisions evolve generally around the
arguments of the participant who has the
greatest stamina and are not necessarily based
on the merits of the case.*

Domestic Meetings

We seem to be unable to conduct any business at all
without having a meeting. This could range from a
casual encounter at the water cooler to a friendly
business lunch. The latter was my favorite since it
combined the necessary with the pleasant. Another
advantage of the business lunch is that it establishes a
tight time frame for the discussion. Finally, it puts the
participants more at ease (who wants to argue on a
full stomach?).

In the business world, there are two basic types of meetings:

1. The meeting to inform or instruct. This could be a group of students getting trained, salesmen being told of the merits of a new gadget to be manufactured, a traveling salesman explaining his wares, or the CEO telling his employees that their company has been profitable, to name a few examples.

2. To resolve issues, gain consensus, and make group decisions. This could involve something quite harmless such as deciding on the color of the walls of the executive washroom or something more relevant such as the amount of alcohol added to a mouthwash product. Activities of standards writing committees or board of directors revolve around such meetings.

This second type of meeting has the biggest impact on how companies are run and, more important, on the bottom line. As mentioned before, in order for CEOs to advance through the company hierarchy from relatively obscure positions, they have to rely more and more on the consensus formed in meetings by their department heads who, quite often, rely in turn on a consensus level input from their own subordinates. (This can lead to an absurd case, where the originator of a top-level company policy directive may be a lowly mail clerk who somehow missed his calling!)

Since group consensus is never created spontaneously, it takes many meetings for a decision to be made.

This then means that the two extreme polarity issues (one that may be truly innovative but daring and the other impractical or absurd) are whittled down to something everybody, or at least most of the members, feel comfortable about. At about the fifth meeting, all but the most persistent advocate of a given issue give up (if for no other reason than sheer boredom) and finally everybody nods his or her head approvingly. Voila! Consensus is achieved.

We all know the adage; "A camel is a race horse designed by committee".... not really a laughing matter. I have known many companies where it is unheard of to have a product developed by responsible individual engineers. The unavoidable consequence of such group design is at best a very mediocre product. One of the more sinister consequences of managing by committee is the subsequent total lack of individual responsibility for a bad policy decision! A committee is a faceless entity; hence, it becomes a comfort factor.

There are, of course, projects that are too big or too multi-disciplined to handle or to understand by a single engineer or scientist. However, clear responsibility should be assigned to cover individual components or portions of the project.

Meetings have evolved into their own culture. There are meetings to plan meetings, meetings to discuss meetings, and don't forget meetings to establish rules for holding meetings. Here are a few names (just add the word *committee*) that most of us are already familiar with: budget, finance, marketing, cost reduction, loss prevention, compensation, safety, environmental, materials, procurement, security, technical steering, standards coordination, computer system, grievance, advisory, management, director, and my favorite...the joint safety, security, and loss prevention committee! Guess what this is: "The Furniture Commodity Strategy Team." Frankly, I don't know either, but I think it has to do with the recycling of used office furniture.

As you can see from the above sampling, there is no single business activity that is immune from our diligent meeting attendees. If we probe deeper, we find there is the dry run or try-out meeting, especially prevalent when preparing for budget meetings. The sole purpose of the meeting is to ensure that all the overheads are in correct order and conform to the party line, and to rehearse the presentations to make sure nothing embarrassing will ever be said in front of the President or Chairman of the Board of Directors.

To define meetings for the purpose of this discussion, what I have in mind is not the chance encounter of two employees at the water cooler nor the habitual meeting of elderly and retired gentlemen at the park bench, but the organized get-together of colleagues at a defined location (conference room 435C), a given time (8:30 a.m.), and a fixed agenda.

The typical day of a middle level manager may start with a 7:00 a.m. breakfast meeting with an out-of-town visitor, followed by the weekly *operations*

70

meetings from 8:00 a.m. to typically 11:00 a.m. At this time he checks his e-mail messages that inform him of meeting schedules for the coming month and specifies his expected contributions. While reviewing his notes, checking his voice mail, and munching on his sandwich for lunch, he is interrupted and told that the scheduled marketing meeting has been rescheduled from 2:00 p.m. to 1:30 p.m. This leaves him barely enough time to collect and sort his overhead slides before dashing again to this next meeting.

The theme here is not so much what the next product should be in order to help improve the company's sagging bottom line, but how to structure the presentation using the latest (and thanks to highly paid consultants) pyramid schema of *added value*. This meeting finally comes to an end at 4:00 p.m. after a very lively debate over the question of whether to use two or three parallel overhead projectors at the upcoming top management presentation (three is the consensus, which poses an intriguing question...which one of the three projected texts should be read aloud?).

Going back to his office, he realizes that he is late for his 4:00 p.m. appointment with his out-of-state visitor who, sure enough, sits patiently before his desk. Apologizing and trying frantically to remember the reason for this visit, the embarrassment is overcome by starting a discussion about the latest winning streak of the local professional baseball team. This, if nothing else, will soon establish the needed

71

camaraderie and spirit of *teamwork* between our hero and the out-of-towner. When the visitor finally leaves at 5:10 p.m., it is time to prepare for the next day, that is, the next day's meetings.

From outward appearances, this has been a very busy day. But you and I may have the nagging question at the back of our minds: What really was accomplished in tangible results? How were sales increased? How was the bottom line (profit)   improved? If it was, probably in some obscure way, it certainly was not measurable and probably out of proportion to the salary paid to our hero (which assumption he certainly will hotly deny).

Unfortunately, the above scenario is no exaggeration, but a daily ritual in our corporate structure. As a quite undesirable by-product (from a social to a health problem point of view), this *meeting mania* has spawned a middle management habit of working an excessive amount of overtime and weekend work. How else can you do the other *productive* assignments you are committed to doing (and, if nothing else, write your presentation paper for the next meeting)? It is common for middle management employees to work 55 to 60 hours a week, not counting travel time.

Just to show to what extent meetings can go, consider the following true story told to me by a very reliable but understandably unnamed source. A corporate budget review was scheduled for November 1. This started frantic staff work in July to prepare the necessary statistical and backup data. About four weeks later, all department managers were requested to incorporate the proposed budget figures into their respective department budgets with a detailed breakdown on the effects of various line items in the budget not only in the coming year but also on the next *five year plan.*

The end of August saw the first of five typically 1-1/2 day *rehearsal* meetings attended by twenty six participants, each having an average of 56 overhead slides. All were neatly tacked along the wall of the oversized conference room for public review and comments by the *team.* Anything not conforming to the *Leitmotiv,* or graphs not presented in the shape of a pyramid, were rejected.

On October 15, after the last rehearsal, which, incidentally, always included reading all the fine text of each slide aloud, everything fell into place. Expected questions from the corporate CEO were posed and *acceptable* answers were rehearsed by everyone (you never knew whom he might ask!). The division president sighed with relief: "We are ready!"

Then a bombshell burst...the budget meeting was postponed to January 3rd. This caused a frantic redirection of effort since, after all, there were now two more operating months to consider. Luckily, the bulk of the presentations could be salvaged; therefore, it was only necessary to hold four additional rehearsals before the big day.

Total *rehearsal* costs alone for the man-hours of the meeting attendees: 2800. This translates into about $140,000 in salaries to which you should add at least $100,000 in staff work and travel expenses.

Of course, one should not overlook the very positive human aspects of meetings. Psychologically, meetings satisfy our *herd* instinct, i.e. the need to belong and interact with a group of our peers. This need becomes more and more important since increasing numbers of office employees are penned up in office cubicles or spend lonely hours in front of computer screens without any face-to-face human interaction. This is a need for *belonging* that has to be satisfied in a healthy office environment. It is a worthy challenge for a good manager to provide effective ways for employees to come together and to satisfy this part of their emotional want while, at the same time, avoiding repeatedly scheduled, time-wasting, and inefficient meeting rituals.

Again, on the positive side of meetings, receiving an invitation to a meeting reinforces your feeling of belonging to a team. In fact, an occasional invitation to a meeting can be used as a reward for work performed well, as an in-between bonus, for example.

Being a regular invitee to a specific meeting, such as weekly cost reviews, makes you a de facto member of a team. It reinforces our longing to be part of a select group very much like our ancestors in the stone age who hunted together, or more recently, like soldiers who fight together in an infantry squad. It instills belonging and camaraderie.

Perhaps time spent in meetings has grown in proportion to the time saved through automation. As an example, the engineering staff in a manufacturing plant used to spend most of their hours doing required engineering calculations for their design work on a slide rule, a task that took perhaps 60% of their time. Later came the electronic pocket calculator that reduced this time to perhaps 45%. We now have computers doing the same chore in split seconds, and even better, we now have software for most of our mathematical routines (eliminating even most of the human thought processes). This reduces the time for engineering calculations that are still required to less than 10% (mostly data input chores).

Let's see, the number of gadgets the company produces is the same and so is the number of engineers. Yet, there is now a time saving of 60% - 10%=50% due to automation. Where does this time go? You guessed it, to be spent in meetings!

International Meetings

So far, I have discussed planned internal or domestic meetings, but there are others on the international level that may well have an impact on our financial well-being. For example, international standards meetings have the lofty ideal of making things worldwide interchangeable. This is generally true only for relatively new technologies that have not seen a billion dollars worth of differently designed and installed base (depending on the nation involved) of gadgets such as the wall outlet for electrical appliances. These are different in practically every country to the chagrin of world travelers.

The unfortunate result of adopting one set of dimensions, over that of another country, is the very high cost of retooling for the *loser* country.

Here is an example: In 1971, when the International Standards Organization (ISO) tried to standardize the installed length of industrial valves, they initially rejected the U.S. proposal for U.S. dimensions on the grounds that U.S. flange pressure ratings were expressed in pounds per square inch. This is a no-no in international standards since everything has to be metric. This writer, then the U.S. delegate to this particular committee, had a bright idea and resubmitted the tabulation under a different heading where he replaced the words *pound per square inch* with the word *class* (i.e., no stated pressures). Thus, a flange rated for 150 psi now was called *Class 150.* This made the U.S. proposal acceptable, and according to *Business Week,** saved the U.S. valve industry $3.5 million in retooling costs. Incidentally, the previously accepted dimensions were taken from the German DIN Standard and would have placed the German valve companies at a significant competitive advantage.

Business Week, pp. 40, (October 7, 1972)

You as a manager or company president may be faced with the question: Should you financially support standard writing activities, or more importantly, send someone of your staff to national or international meetings extending perhaps over as much as 10 years? Before you decide this perhaps costly question, make sure such activity is clearly in the interest of your company or your industry and that it ultimately will help to sell your products.

Next, consider the cost. Writing a standard typically takes 4 to 10 years, totaling between 800 to 2000 man-hours for each delegate. This translates to $40000 to $100000 of salary and related expenses plus, perhaps another $15000 to $50000 of travel expenses. Therefore, carefully study the subject yourself since nobody will give you the straight facts.

There are other, perhaps more subtle influences from abroad, on our business. Examples are Supra National Committees such as the Trilateral Commission, which was chaired for many years by David Rockefeller (of Chase Manhattan Bank), still very much influences the political relationship between the U.S., Europe, Japan, and the *Club of Rome*,[*] which in 1972 decreed that the rate of consumption in the developing countries would lead to disaster and early depletion of raw materials. As a result, we have environmental movements, lead free gasoline, catalytic converters in cars, and a substantial growth in government bureaucracy willfully enlarged to create additional

[*] *The Economist*, pp. 19 (December 20, 1997)

purchasing power to absorb the excess industrial production capacity in the hope of avoiding disruptive business cycles.

What to do about meetings.

There are numerous ways to increase the efficiency of meetings such as by shortening their duration and by running meetings in a more businesslike manner (having a good chairperson). According to Milo C. Frank[*], "The difference between a stimulating discussion and a productive meeting is results!"

The best way to run meetings is to have none! The second best way is to have as few as possible. Decisions should be made by the CEO or department heads following input and/or advice from his or her subordinates, but never by a unanimous committee vote. This way he or she can take full credit for a good decision or full blame for a bad one. This is the way it should be.

Why do I discuss meetings at great length? Because in a corporate structure they contribute more than anything else to highly wasteful allocation and use of mostly salaried labor, and to bad business decisions. While decisions derived in committees create consensus (which may be positive), the consensus is derived after considerable time....time that in our ever-faster business cycles becomes a rare

---

[*] Frank, Milo C., "How to run a successful meeting in half the time," (New York: Simon & Schuster, 1989).

commodity. Most Japanese companies were known to run their businesses by the consensus method. That is no longer true. More and more companies can no longer afford this luxury and have discarded this relic from the past. And don't even confuse meetings derived consensus with *teamwork*. While it takes a football *team* to win a game, it is still the individual team member who kicks the field goal!

Here is a tip, when you *must* have a safety or loss prevention committee (because some state governments mandate it), (a) have as few people as possible participate, and (b) try to have this committee meet only once a year!

As to the number of participants, being a member of a committee is for many people a matter of great prestige, especially when selected from the lower ranks. Therefore, they will do their best to come up with many *solutions* to prove their mettle.

The other problem is meeting sequence. When the committee starts, it is easy to find the obvious shortcomings like, "there is no lighted exit sign over the rear door of warehouse 1," or "the safety guard on the belt sander is broken." However, after the second or third monthly meeting, members are hard pressed to find flaws. Since committees *never* voluntarily disband, and because it looks silly to have minutes of meetings showing no tangible results, problems are invented so solutions can be found! Such as, "let's relocate door No. 2 in Building C so that in case of a fire, we can shorten the escape route." After all, the human mind, and if you have ten members, up to ten human minds, can be very resourceful when it comes to proving its need for existence on this committee.

Now management is between a rock and a hard place. Giving into many superfluous and costly solutions will drain the maintenance staff's labor and will cost a lot of money. To refuse will open up the company to the possibility of a future lawsuit in case, God forbid, some accident happens and the plaintiff's lawyer can prove that management *willfully ignored* most recommendations of the safety committee. You can almost see the angry reaction of any jury to such callous behavior!

The other detriment of ignoring committee recommendations is the adverse results on the morale of the employees. Therefore, meeting ideally only once a year reduces the number of problems faced by management by a factor of twelve, yet everybody stays happy!

Of course, in the *good old days* before intervention of the all-knowing and all-caring government, you had an inspector from your insurance company come around maybe once a year. He was a trained professional, and he would spot shortcomings, write a report, and management would fix the problem(s) if required. Alas, we don't live in such simple times anymore! We have to do our best to live with the facts of modern life.

Hey, here is a great idea! How about a committee to study and limit the adverse effects of other committees on the fiscal well-being of your company?

A final note: Volunteer as a secretary of a committee (chairman being the first choice) if you want to influence the outcome of committee deliberations. That way you can write the committee minutes the way <u>you</u> feel the discussion went on important issues.

Chapter 7

Budgets

Many a bonus for meeting or exceeding a budget
would have been missed where it not for the
effects of inflation.

Let me explain the above statement. All corporate management (and shareholders) want a company to grow; ergo, the pressure on the sales department to increase its sales goal for the next year by say at least 5% over the actual sales of the current year. Such a goal, typically for companies with mature product lines, may comprise a 2% planned price increase and a 3% rate of "penetration," i.e., you think you can grow 3% by taking this amount away from your competitor. The latter may not happen, especially if business is slow. Yet, you still exceeded the budget by 2% because of your price increase. This means your sales manager will still get a bonus for exceeding last year's sales figures not because of his special effort but simply due to inflation. Price increases are really an adjustment for inflation. While your dollar sales grew by 2%, the number of gadgets sold by your company did not!

While it is typical for mature industries to set a 5% goal to increase sales, rapidly growing hi-tech companies may set goals of up to 100% increase per year, at least until their competitors catch up.

How to establish a yearly operating budget

If you are already in business, the first thing to look at is last year's actual performance, or at least a good portion of last year's actual figures. Since the typical request for next year's operating budget arrives six months before the end of the business year, you simply multiply the six-month figures available from the current year by two. This procedure may have to be adjusted if you have a very seasonable business. For example, if you sell or manufacturer 30% more in October (by past experience), then multiply the 2 × six-month data by $1 + (30^*/12 \times 100) = 1.025$. For instance, if you sold $6 million worth of goods from January through the end of July, and you expect to sell $1 million + 30% = $1.3 million in October, then your projected sales for the year will be $2 \times 6 \times (1 + 30/12 \times 100) = \$12.3$ million.

---

* The percentage increase per month, (for example, if you expect a 30% increase during 2 months out of a year use 2x30 = 60. This then makes the multiplier 1.05).

83

It is also customary to add any contemplated price increase, for example, to nullify the effects of inflation on your cost of sales. Again, this should be pro-rated. For example, if your fiscal year starts in January and you want to increase prices by 3% on the first of April, then your total budgeted yearly sales volume should be increased by 3% × 9 months/12 months = 2.25%.

So much for the expected revenues; now for the expenses. The cost of goods sold should be easy. This should not vary much as a percentage of sales (say 53%), so you use the same percentage as in the prior year. The difference (47% of sales) is your gross profit. Note your gross profit may be up to 85 % if you happened to own a software company.

The next step is to consider your fixed expenses such as rent, utilities, interest on loan payments, fees for accountants, depreciation of automobiles, etc., which may equal 17%. This leaves you with about 30% for salaries, wages, travel and communication expenses, *and* profit.

Say you want to be left with a 10% profit on sales before tax. This means that your personnel, travel, and communication expenses cannot exceed 20% of sales. This is the hardest part to work on because it is the most difficult to fix. For example, you have to guess beforehand how much of a raise you will give your employees during the coming year. Using the previous example, if your payroll is 17% of gross sales and you want to give an average increase of 4%,

84

your profit will shrink by 17% × 4%/100 = 0.68%, i.e., the profit is 10% - 0.68% = 9.32% instead of 10%. In most companies, salaries and wages can affect over 80% of the profit. Personnel have the most important impact on profitability.

Remember that a yearly budget is only a rough financing guideline to your future. It may need to be adjusted at least on a quarterly basis, especially when a recession strikes. Sometimes reducing inventory and laying off people is the only available remedy to avoid red ink, or worse, bankruptcy.

Table 7-1, is an example of a typical operating budget for a fictitious XYZ Corporation. The current year projects a total sales volume of $25,296,000 million and it is contemplated that sales will increase by 18.6% to $30 million. Note the net profit for the current year is only $1.27 million or 5% of sales. Besides cost of sales at 50%, the other big-ticket items are commissions at 10.4% and wages and last year's salaries at 10.4%. You cannot do anything about the commission since this is a contractual obligation, so let us concentrate on personnel expenses. By not hiring new employees in proportion to the projected increase in sales, you can slash the proposed increase in salaries to 10 % (A) instead of the 18.6% following the sales increase. This also slows the increase in employee benefits (B), pension plus bonuses (C) and employment related taxes (D). Now you managed to bump up the net profit from 5% to 7.1% of sales, (a 42% increase), or $848,700 more in the bank!

This is effective indeed and practically the *only* way to increase profitability. With an increase in sales, your managers will resist you less in slowing the hiring of personnel. The problem is much more acute if sales slow down. All the managers will resist letting go of their people--a real challenge. Notice that direct labor (effective employees) typically increases directly and proportionally with sales, so there is no problem. We are talking about restricting the growth of the "supportive employees" as elsewhere defined, or more bluntly, in overhead!

If the complaints about "too much workload" get too loud, offer the option to work overtime. You will be amazed how much the "excess work load" gets resolved by this threat, realizing that most salaried employees do not get paid overtime.

Budgets

Table 7-1
XYZ Corp
Operating Budget in $1,000

	Next Year	% of Sales	Current Year	% of Sales
SALES	$30,000	100	$25,296	100
COST OF SALES				
Cost of Sales, Labor	9,750	32.5	8,259	32.5
Cost of Sales, Material	5,250	17.5	4,431	17.5
Total Cost of Sales	15,000	50	12,690	50
Gross Profit	15,000	50	12,606	50
OPERATING EXPENSES				
Travel	300	1.0	272.9	1.1
Telephone & Communication	100	0.3	88.0	0.3
Product Liability Insurance	60	0.2	58.1	0.2
Advertising	300	1.0	232.6	1
Web Site	60	0.2	62	0.3
Commissions	3,124	10.4	2,634.1	10.4
Shipping	300	1	267.4	1
(A)Wages & Salaries (other than labor)	2,900	9.7	2,638.2	10.4
(C) Bonus	53	1.8	48.0	2
Pension	176	0.6	160	0.6
Consultants	700	2.3	600	2.4
(D)Employer FICA	300	1	287.9	1.1
(D)State Unemployment Tax	14	-	13.4	-
(D) Federal Unemployment Tax	18	-	16.3	-
Directors Expense	42	0.1	36	0.1
(B) Employee Benefits	318	1.1	268.6	1.1
Utilities	760	2.5	64.2	2.5
Real Estate Taxes	110	0.3	100	0.4
General Insurance	60	0.2	59.3	0.2
Factory Supplies	100	0.3	91.6	0.3
Building Maintenance	50	0.2	46	0.2
Depreciation	260	1	250.2	1
Dues & Subscriptions	12	-	14.7	-
Offices Supplies	60	0.2	52.4	0.2
Legal & Accounting	120	0.4	97.0	0.4
Research & Development	600	2	554.0	2.2
Interest & Sundry Expense	700	2.3	685.7	2.7
Auxiliary Labor	30	0.1	22.5	0.1
Total General, Administrative & Selling Expenses	10,943	36.5	9721.1	38.4
Income from Operations	4,057	13.5	2,884.9	11.4
Interest Expenses	(1,200)	(4.0)	(1,100)	(4.3)

(Continued on next page)

87

(Continued)	Next Year	% of Sales	Current Year	% of Sales
OTHER INCOME				
Interest & Sundry Income	150	0.5	128.4	0.5
Royalty Income	60	0.2	55	0.2
Total Other Income	210		183.4	
Income Before Income Taxes	3,277	10.9	1,968.3	7.8
Income Taxes - State	175	0.6	105	0.4
Income Taxes - Federal	980	3.2	590	2.3
NET INCOME	2,122	7.1	1,273.3	5.0

Planning for capital expenditures

If times were good during the past year and you wound up with some extra cash in your bank account, then you want to set up a capital budget. This expenditure is to ensure further growth or to replace worn or obsolete equipment such as computers with insufficient random access memories (at least that is what your employees will tell you!).

As to the amount to set aside, this depends on how fast your business is growing. If you need new shop and office space, plus new equipment, substantial amounts of money can be acquired by going to your local bank for a collateralized loan, or if a publicly held corporation, you may float (sell) more stock in your company. Other ways to preserve cash in these circumstances is leasing buildings and equipment (see also chapter on "Chasing The Rainbow or How To Get Started").

If, on the other hand, you are in a mature business, then your capital expenditures are relatively low and should not exceed your amount of depreciation on your present equipment, buildings, and automobiles. There is a tendency by management to be more tolerant when it comes to approving capital expenditures than to give an okay for a worldwide advertising campaign, for example. The reasons are simple. Advertising is an expense and directly reduces the profit on a one-to-one basis. A capital expenditure only reduces available cash and affects profit only in a minor way; first by paying higher interest expenses (if the cash came via a bank loan, or losing interest if cash came from other investments) and second, by increasing the amount of depreciation. So instead of a $100,000 advertising expenditure reducing profits by $100,000, a capital addition of $100,000 will reduce profit by only perhaps $12,000. Nevertheless, all capital expenditures should be scrutinized just as much as direct expenditures.

Pay special attention to moneys left over in a capital appropriation budget towards the end of the year. A lot of cash happens to be wasted here.

It is an absolute horror to mid-level management to have unspent money in a given capital expenditure budget. The horror, of course, is that if there is money left over, then next year's capital budget will invariably be cut. This leaves you with a problem. If you spent less this year, you may not get enough money for next year even though you may really need the higher capital budget because of "real" increases in business. A more serious concern is that this surplus (unspent capital funds) exposes you as a bad planner and an incapable business manager who was unable to correctly forecast your budget needs during the prior year. The easy solution is to avoid such an embarrassment by spending "willy-nilly" the rest of the allocated budget during the last days of the business year. Your vendors will love you and none of your superiors will be the wiser. Incidentally, this quite common behavior explains the yearly phenomenal increase in sales volume by equipment manufacturers during the last two weeks of December.

Remember this: *"The need to spend moneys out of capital budgets increases in proportion to the time that is left until the year-end."* Don't get sucked into this because capital spending does not directly affect the company's profit. **It is still money!**

Chapter 8

The Computer And Other
Forms of Miscommunication

The sum of all communication is zero.

The above may sound like a paradox, but it is not. For every message we send out, we expect an answer (at least in theory), bringing the total outstanding messages to zero.

Today, it seems incomprehensible to think World War II was won without a computer, let alone a fax machine or even a simple office copy machine. But it was with an incredible amount of personnel (16.1 million[*]) and material being moved in two separate

---

[*] *Statistical Abstract of the United States,* (Washington DC: U.S. Department of Commerce, 1996).

parts of the world. The question is, could we duplicate this feat with the vast amount of information technology at our disposal today? The answer is not necessarily an unqualified *yes*.

Another example is mail delivery. All the automatic sorting equipment and computer systems cannot guarantee same day first class letter delivery say between Boston and New York--a feat that was accomplished with hand sorting and steam locomotives 100 years ago. What we have to realize is that the increase in *information* demands has caused an increase in personnel to handle it, i.e., create and disseminate the information.

E-Mail Mania

In the past, you wrote a letter to Department A, perhaps with a copy to your boss (the number of legible copies a typewriter could handle was definitely limited.) Today, with a click of a button, e-mail allows you to send a letter to the person the letter is addressed to as well as to a great number of other people simultaneously.

Why do we do it other than because *it is so easy*? First, it shows the world that we are doing our job; secondly, we somehow expect a reply *from other interested parties*, even from as far away as Katmandu! The result is a vast proliferation of e-mail messages which all have to be read because you may be the person to whom it is addressed instead of merely being copied.

Two problems now arise: First, employees spend a great portion of their supposedly productive hours doing *electronic communication.* Secondly, if people are too busy being productive, as they should be, they ignore e-mail. This is not necessarily good either because there may have been an important and urgent request lurking among the fluff. By in large more and more people write and read e-mail (with gradually increasing grammar and spelling errors if education progresses on its current path). They do this primarily out of fear of appearing computer illiterate or old fashioned. The invariable result is an increase in the total office work hours, or translated, more employees.

Under the headlines, "A flood of messages is inundating offices," The *Wall Street Journal**reported on a study sponsored by Pitney Bowes, Inc., which found that e-mail is not replacing other kinds of messages but is *layered over existing methods, increasing the communication load.* They go on to report that some people get more than 150 messages a day! At three minutes each, that adds 7.5 hours to a working day! So where does such a person find time to answer the phone, attend meetings, and lastly, but **most importantly,** do some productive work! What invariably will happen is that such a person will

---

* *Wall Street Journal*, Tuesday, April 8, 1997, P. B1.

delegate some of his or her responsibilities. In plain English, he or she will hire an assistant.

According to *Business NH Magazine of January 1999,* there are 102 million corporate e-mail boxes in service worldwide, and that usage is growing by 60% per year. Frankly, I am not that pessimistic.

First of all, the novelty is beginning to wear off. Secondly, persons who in the past were too lazy to write a letter will keep the same habits when it comes to e-mail. What is perhaps more troublesome, and in the end more expensive due to the electronic storage space involved, is the proliferation of *Attachments* to the e-mail, which can include very large files including graphic arts, which place extraordinary demands on the message infrastructure. Proper training and placing restrictions on the use of e-mail may be in order.

As much as the fax machine displaced the telex machine, e-mail is now displacing the fax machine. I still think it is much easier to fax a document then to scan it into your computer, make a file, dial your service provider, and send the file as an e-mail attachment. Then again I may not do it the modern way. Nevertheless, the above points to the fact that management needs to establish reasonable rules about the use of the Internet. Better yet, try to keep your employees busy with productive work!

So much for the bad news, now to the good news. What we will see in the future is a balanced and efficient utilization of all our communication devices in parallel, whether it is the phone, the postal service, fax, video, or computer, since each of these devices has some important advantages for given specific tasks over the other ones.

After e-mail started to flourish, companies decided to eliminate secretarial positions. After all, who needs a secretary if the manager can type his own e-mail? It may be a seemingly justifiable reason for having e-mail with the resultant personnel (secretary) savings. However, I suspect otherwise. First of all, only departments or senior management had secretaries and there are, perhaps, 10 e-mail users for each terminated secretarial position. Secondly, if a manager with a $100,000 a year salary types (probably one finger method) his own mail, which may take an average of two hours per day, this will cost his company about $25,000 per year. Compared to the salary of a secretary, it is not much of a saving not counting the more productive work the manager could have been performing during the time he was typing.

The greatest accomplishment of Bill Gates and others like him was, in my opinion, to make it fashionable for presidents of large corporations to type their own letters. Ten years ago they would have thrown you out of their offices if you dared make such a suggestion. Just to show you how ridiculous e-mail mania has become, one only needs to look around to see that people send e-mail messages to each other even though their offices are within shouting distance!

95

A related item is the *Internet*. Here we see a mixture of quite legitimate use such as getting quotes, and looking up potential vendors, and personal misuse by employees. As stated in a software advertisement published in the June 5, 2000. issue of the *FINANCIAL TIMES*, "up to 59 percent of business use is not business related!". This may be somewhat exaggerated after all this advertiser wants to sell software capable of preventing abuse, but then again not far from the truth. This misuse is not so much computer related but rather a loss of productive time of the employee involved. In my own experience, the majority of employees who p*lay* on the Internet do it out of sheer boredom, not having enough to do. Therefore, this problem cannot be solved by adding yet another software to prevent access, but rather by better supervision and more workload allocation by the supervisor.

Then, of course, the problem may lie deeper and we may discover that a particular department where most Internet abuses occur is overstaffed. However, the manager in charge will never admit this. Nevertheless, here is a case where top management, via Internet monitoring can spot opportunities for manpower pruning in order to improve the bottom line.

Now to a technical problem: Have you ever wondered why, especially during the busy working hours, your computer dialed and dialed and no connection? When you finally got connected it took forever for the *hourglass symbol* to disappear on your screen so you could read your message. It is not happening because your microprocessor is too slow, or that you don't have enough random access memory. Rushing out and buying a new computer does not solve this problem.

What most of us don't understand is that your local *server*, i.e., the device that gets a phone call from your computer asking for data input is overloaded. First, there is a limit on the number of calls that a server can handle at any given time. If this number is exceeded, then the server simply does not connect. But instead of telling you *the line is busy* it gives you the message *connection failed, check your password*, or similarly misleading information to keep you confused.

Secondly, even if you finally get connected (after the 15th ring), getting data on the screen is frustratingly slow. Why? Because now the server divides your time with that of the other users *calling in*. This is a process called *multiplexing*. Say there are 30 PCs calling a server simultaneously. The server computer allocates $1/30^{th}$ of a minute to transmit data to each of the connected PCs. You can watch this on your screen. The bright flickering of light on the tiny simulated screens indicates you are getting, or transmitting data from our to your server. The pauses (usually too long) with no light indicate that somebody else is being served at that moment. The pauses between *data bursts* get longer the more users ask for data at the same time. So you can see, there is nothing wrong

97

with your PC; there is just simply insufficient server capacity. Try to connect late in the evening, and you will be amazed how fast your computer suddenly becomes!

Phone tag or other office fun

The good old telephone, which served us so well for more than 100 years, is getting *modernized*, i.e., adding to the *efficiency* of the office. Ten years ago you could call the sales manager of a vendor company and the company operator would courteously connect you to him. If he were on a trip or in a meeting, you would get to speak to his secretary who would then take a message or would let you know when he would be available. That is no longer true. Now you talk to a computer that asks you to enter the first three letters of a person's last name! In most cases, you would not know the sales manager's name (unless you look it up in the Dow Jones® Index). Even if you knew the name, you may be apt to misspell it and not get a connection, or the directory list may not be current.... after all, under which job description does phone system programmer/manager fall? Finally, if you are lucky, you may get into his voice mail.

The latter is a fiendish invention by the telephone companies to add untold billions of dollars to their revenues for unneeded and wasteful telephone services.

Voice Mail is nothing but a sexier name for *answering service*. Since the secretary disappeared with the coming of the age of e-mail, there would be no one to tell you that the person you are seeking to talk to may be on vacation, sick, on a trip, in a meeting, *indisposed*, or fired. What is worse is, that people have gotten so used to having voice mail, they don't even bother to answer the phone when it rings in their office. When they later (if ever) return the call, chances are they only get the voice mail of the first caller, thereby playing a *catch-me* game to the huge delight and profit of the telephone companies!

How to communicate effectively.

You are confronted with a number of choices of how to communicate in a modern office environment. The question is, which is most cost effective, and hence less time consuming. Most of us tend to concentrate on the latest "gizmo" while neglecting other forms of well-proven and established technologies. This does not have to be that way. Try to evaluate your needs from both the standpoint of convenience *and* efficiency since no system is ideal. Well, here is a comparison:

    1. Verbal communication. Be it a one-on-one conversation, a discussion during a meeting, or, an informative talk to a group of employees, this is by far the most effective way of communicating. Another advantage is that you can get instant feedback through questions posed by your

listener(s). A possible drawback is that the size of the company or number of people involved limits this. One of the reasons why smaller companies (less than 100 employees) tend to be more efficient is no doubt the ability of management to talk to each employee. So, unless he is your sworn enemy, do talk to your neighbor in the office next to you, rather than send him e-mail, even if it is not "cool".

2. By telephone. This lacks some of the spontaneity of the face-to-face discussion (video conferencing still has its limits). While it lacks the ability to observe the facial expressions, or, the body language of your talking partners which are very important inputs to observe, especially when you are negotiating, this is still my number two choice.

3. By video conferencing. This is less personal than a face-to-face meeting and in some ways superior over the telephone conference where you sometimes don't know who is speaking at a given moment. However it requires special rooms and really needs a camera operator to be truly effective. I was in a videoconference with a fixed camera focusing on the seated chairman of our firm, when suddenly he decided to get up. The rest was a monologue conducted by a pair of legs.

4. E-Mail. This can be a very effective way of communication especially among several people. But it is a written form that lacks spontaneity and

which is subject to the same limitations as faxes and letters. Other drawbacks are informality and lack of electronic software standards when it comes to transmission and readability of attachments. Finally, there is a tendency to copy too many people which is time consuming for them and therefore inefficient.

5. Facsimile. This form of electronic data transmission is loosing favor compared to e-mail. Don't discard it yet. It is much easier and faster to feed a document into a fax machine than to scan it, start a file, and then transfer it to e-mail, unless it goes to a number of recipients.

6. Letters. This is a somewhat more permanent and legally more binding way of communicating. It still has its place if formality is desired, especially in contract work.

7. Finally, there is the telegram. This still allows for speedy communication with people in certain foreign countries and, or, without access to computers or fax machines.

While the above comparison is meant for an office environment, different means such as cell-phones and hand-held communication devices are a must when you are on the road. Every traveler who ever lugged his portable computer over miles of walkways in airports can readily appreciate the soon universally available portable phones having the ability to read his e-mail while away from the office.

Data explosions

Now onto computers. Computers do a vital task without which we could not support most operations in accounting, engineering, planning, etc. The trouble is computers need software, i.e., a specific set of instructions to perform a given task. Here is where the trouble begins. Software costs make or break an operation. They can perform virtual miracles and create reams of useful data, or they can create chaos requiring endless re-education of workers, constant monitoring and maintenance because of system *crashes*, and, otherwise, can be a bottomless pit in which management spends endless amounts of money to get either different software or hire consultants. A love-hate relationship exists in many companies regarding computer systems. With computer hardware becoming more and more complex, we need System Managers to keep our PC-networks and software running properly, a position that did not exist 15 years ago.

Billion-dollar chip and computer industries exist primarily because they convince us that we always need more memory, or yet, a more powerful computer model. As Marshall McLuhan proclaimed, "The media is the message." The perceived *payback* of capital invested for computers in the eyes of management is to save labor. That is, the expended funds will be recovered in personnel savings. Sadly, this is seldom true.

As pointed out by Stephen Roach[*], a Morgan Stanley analyst, there is no evidence that computers actually save labor, taking the economy as a whole! He states that the productivity gains of the information age are just a myth. I can attest to this based on my own, albeit limited, experience. The reason for this seemingly irrational finding is quite simple. In the past, when we compiled statistics or reports by hand using only adding machines, the output was rather limited and the reporting activity was restricted, say, to a monthly P&L statement and a sales statistic, for example. The computer made it easy to add many more reports. System managers, typically beg their *customers* (company department heads) for requests for even more reports to be generated. The reason is simple: having more requests will increase his or her department and stature in the company. I recall one sales manager who requested a monthly sales report on not only what was sold but to whom, including the exact nature of the customer's business, the location, and so on. In small print, this monthly report would be 3 inches thick. The Data Handling Department always placed a new report on the vice president's credenza to be removed next month to make space for the newer report. I never recall seeing him read this report. In any case, it would have taken him several days to do so. He quite simply requested the report because *it could be done*. I am sure he has no idea

---

[*] *New Hampshire Sunday News*, Manchester, New Hampshire, August 17, 1997.

how much money it cost his company to compile, store, maintain, and process all that data.

Excess investment in automation, of which data systems is part, can lead to a drain in financial resources and efficiencies. If overhead becomes excessive, try to force your competitors to follow your example (and become equally inefficient), otherwise you will find yourself to be no longer competitive and out of business.

A case in point: After supermarkets became the predominant place to do one's shopping, it forced practically all local *mom and pop* grocery stores out of business. That was in the 1960s and 1970s. Since then, supermarkets have invested heavily in automating their inventory control and checkout systems (most notably barcode reading equipment). The result was a steady escalation of grocery prices to pay for the required extra capital.

The unforeseen and surprising results are that local convenience stores are back in business and are thriving!

In his book, *The Great Boom Ahead*[*], Harry Dent states: "We have put computers to work to make our huge bureaucratic staffs a little more efficient with word processing, accounting with financial spreadsheets, and so on! The least investment has

---

[*] Dent, Harry, *The Great Boom Ahead*, (New York: Hyperion, 1993).

gone into our sales and customer service personnel, the very people who affect our customers the most. This is why our investments in computerization in the 70s and 80s produced such minor productivity gains." Well said, and may I add, "--- in the 90s too!"

To most of you my comments sound too pessimistic. The young readers weaned on marketing hype from computer and software salesmen will even consider me as being completely out of touch and misinformed, while older, experienced readers may nod their heads knowingly. Be as it may, the sad fact is that I have not encountered or read about any improvement in overall plant productivity with the aid of computers. When I say this I mean, of course, the use of the computer in running everything from order entry to inventory, the so called *Enterprise System* and not a computerized machine tool or robot, for example, where the computer has indeed greatly improved productivity.

Support in my assessment comes, for example, from a recent article by Paul A. Strassmann[*] who states that of 1,848 randomly selected corporations reviewed, the ratio of company assets to total revenue increased dramatically since computers became widely used in the management of companies.

As shown in Figure 8-1, the assets that were used to produce revenue increased 175% in the time span ranging from 1982 to 1999. In other words, if it took

---

[*] Strassman, Paul E., DIET? WHAT DIET?, *ComputerWorld*, September 20, 2001.

$129 million of assets (plant, tools, computers, servers, inventory, etc.) to produce $100 million in sales, it took $226 million in invested assets to produce the same sales volume in 1999! This is quite shocking to think about and it speaks poorly of utilization of shareholder values.

As Strassmann says: "A long held favorite assumption about computerization is that the more you have, the fewer corporate assets you need. But a look at corporate data suggests that the opposite has happened since 1982".

Perhaps the picture may not be as bad as indicated since part of the increase in assets used may be due to the use of more expensive (but more efficient) machine tools for example. However, I think nobody can make a case for the opposite argument, which is computer systems increase efficiency in plant operations.

Why is this? First of all there are too many computers used throughout a plant and there are too many (mostly unread) reports generated. Remember that in 1982 a typical factory had only three mainframe computers for sales, inventory control, and finance. Now it has hundreds of personal computers (with their own printers), several servers, additional mainframes, and, of course a large IT department. However, the real bugaboo is that poor software packages are being designed and purchased without clear understanding what the operation or organization really needs. For more on this subject see the next chapter.

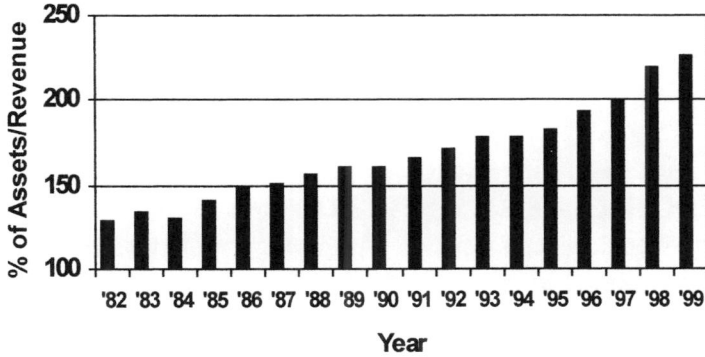

Figure 8-1: Percent of assets needed to produce 100% of Revenue(Sales).

Chapter 9

Computer Software

*Advances in computer programming barely keep up with
the increase in illiteracy of the general population.*

Software is to computers what gasoline is to
automobiles--without it, nothing runs. Aside from
general software programs that allow you to type a
letter or set up a simple balance sheet, managers of
companies need very sophisticated programs that can
run an entire company operation including sales, order
entry, manufacturing, engineering, purchasing, and
accounting just to name a few basic departments
(sometimes called an Enterprise System).

The function of each of these departments, or
functional blocks within a company organization,
usually evolved over many years of growth and
continual adjustments to hopefully make it more
efficient and productive. This all added some

complexity to the organization. The result is that very few people, if any, can tell you the exact workflow, the reasons for doing certain things, and explain the overall departmental system. If things get that complicated on the department level, what do you think happens on the overall company level with perhaps 12 to 15 departments? There is probably no CEO alive who can explain the exact route a customer order takes from the incoming fax, e-mail, or call to the invoice being mailed to the customer.

You now expect an outside software company to duplicate this system, which exists only in the heads of perhaps 100 different people, and to put it into programming language for a company-wide computer system. This is practically an impossible task and exactly the crux of the problem encountered by many CEOs, which brought many companies to the brink of bankruptcy.

There are only two ways of automating company-wide systems. The first, and preferred way, is to purchase good, commercially available software that is able to combine word processing and data-handling capabilities. You then use a bright software engineer, preferably from your own company (so he is familiar the way your company works), and have him modify or adapt this canned software to duplicate as much as possible the exact way your individual departments currently operate. It is absolutely essential to establish exactly what the software should do *before* any software coding begins. This should be done in writing with everybody concerned signing off on it.

Resist all temptations to load-up the software with unnecessary reports and functions! Unfortunately, doing only this much is already quite complex and you may only be able to do it by individual departments. Nevertheless, try to set the software up so it can accept data input from one department to the next (saving redundancy thereby cutting costs and errors). If everything goes well, you eventually have a company-wide data processing system that runs smoothly and requires hardly any training of the people involved. After all, they are doing the same work as before except now they are working on a PC or workstation instead of doing it by, say, a typewriter or individual PCs. Nevertheless, even this takes lots of time and training.

It is absolutely essential that you do not switch over from a manual to a computer system immediately. Work both systems in parallel for at least six months. Make sure the program is thoroughly debugged. Even if things run smoothly, don't discard the old manual forms or typewriters quite yet. They may come in handy when the system crashes.

The above, in my opinion, is the only way to computerize a company system; however, there is another way. This typically is an evolved enterprise system, which not only requires elaborate hardware but also requires very expensive software. The six or seven digit software cost is only the tip of the iceberg. According to an article in the *Wall Street Journal**[*]

---

[*] *Wall Street Journal*, March 14, 1997, p. B1.

describing a popular German R/3(software program: "Companies must play host to armies of consultants who sometimes charge as much as five times what the software itself cost and can stay on the job for years." They cite Owens-Corning Fiberglass Corp. for paying between $15 to $20 million for their R/3 project.

The above-mentioned consultants are needed for explaining to and training your employees on how the new system works. You have to understand that in order to use such software, you have to adapt the way you used to do business to the new way dictated by the outside system. This is tantamount to redesigning your company from the ground up....everything runs differently.

It involves months of organizational upheaval, shuffling of personnel, untold near or actual nervous breakdowns, vast amounts of costly man hours due to retraining, and so on. This also does not include the lost orders, reduced company image, upset customers, etc.

Municipal governments are even bigger victims of what sometimes amounts to software fraud. As a headline in the March 21, 1997 issue of the *Palm Beach Post* reported: "Unneeded software cost the county $2.8 million including $1.04 million on maintenance."

Alas, if everything is done right after spending untold millions of dollars, at the touch of a button the CEO will now know the up to the second amounts of orders in house. Wow!

One thing you have to realize is the sophisticated software programs discussed above tend to revolve around the Accounting Department and its requirements (see Fig. 9-1). No wonder, because some of the software programs were created by accounting firms such as Price-Waterhouse. To me, this is a perversion of the order of importance. By far the most important portion of any manufacturing organization is order fulfillment, or the manufacturing system (see Fig. 9-2). If this system works well, your customers are happy and you make a profit.

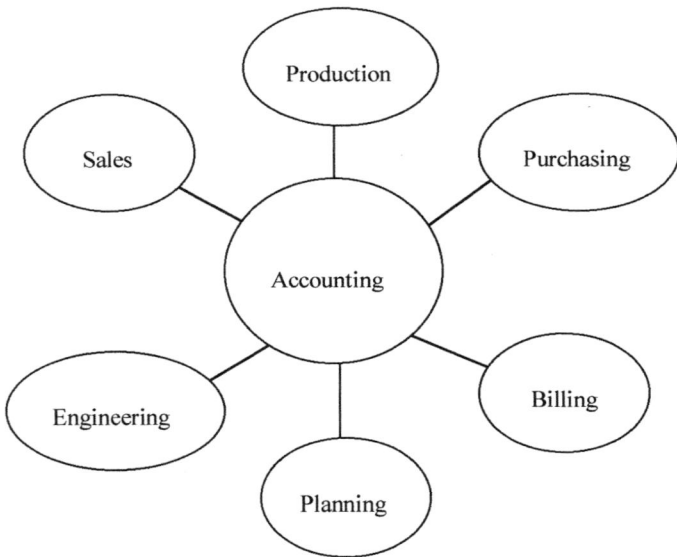

Figure 9-1: Example of accounting-centered enterprise software.

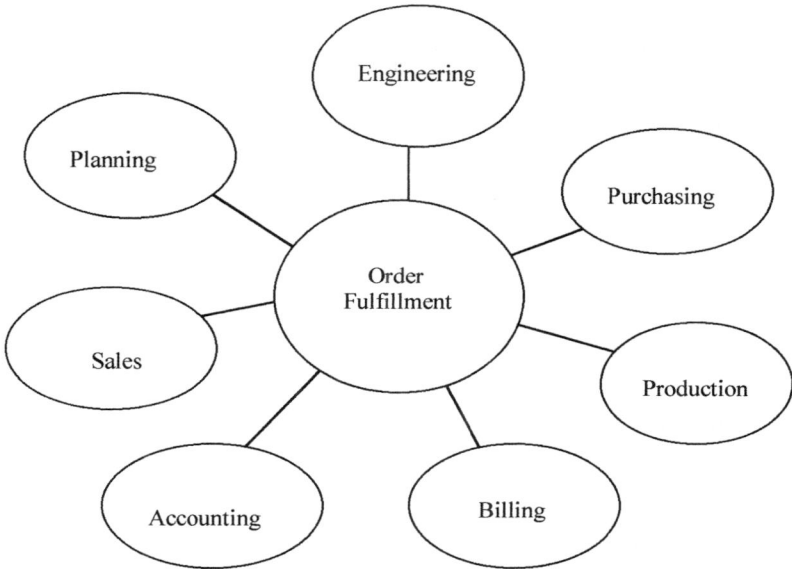

Figure 9-2: A more rational manufacturing system-centered enterprise software.

To balance the books is of secondary importance. If everything else fails, you can always call your banker and see if the cash in your bank account is growing--- a sure sign that you are making money. If not, then you are in trouble with or without fancy software.

113

There is the tempting logic to center software around the accounting requirements. After all, nearly everything can be expressed in terms of money (cost, inventory, sales, etc.). However, such a system will certainly force you to redesign all of your company's vital operations in order to comply with the demands of such software.

I know of a pump company who used a standard cost system in the past that consisted of groups of product lines and sizes with some adjustments for variations thrown in. This cost accounting system was so effective, that the difference between the book value and the inventory to the value of the physical count was always less than 1%!

The new software program required that a different Bill of Material* be generated for each, separate pump (even if it differed from a "standard" pump by only a primer coat). The result was an excess of 10,000 bills of materials and still counting. The only persons not complaining about this waste of money are the new employees hired to generate all these new documents.

On the other hand, a production-centered software program allows you to adapt and keep your present system more or less intact.

---

* A listing of separate parts required to build a complete assembly, in this case, a pump.

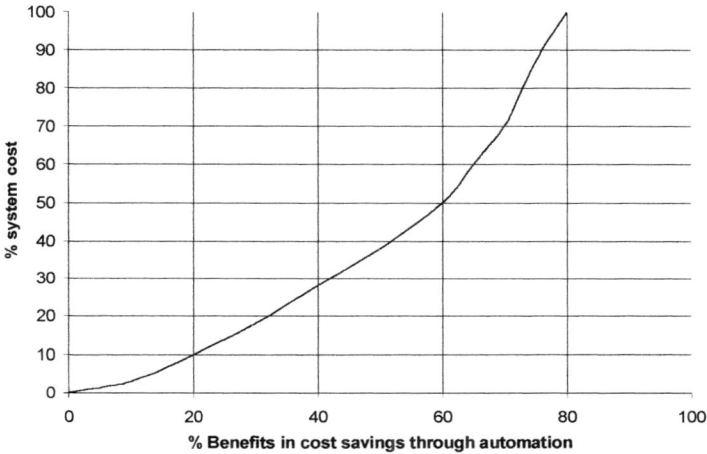

Figure 9-3 - Typical Cost Benefit Relationship between computer plus software cost and percentage of perceived benefits through system automation. Note: At 80%, benefits cost already exceeds 100%! Optimal benefits lie around 60%. Don't ever try to reach 100% automation.

Chapter 10

Running An Enterprise Government Style

Taxes expand to cover Government's Losses.

We may belittle inefficient government agencies or enterprises when they are run so badly because it has been reported so often that we are numb to it. It is true that any inefficiency will always be covered up by tax money, contrary to private enterprise where bankruptcy is the inevitable end of such folly (except if a business has a monopoly in a given service or product). In the latter case, a price increase will cover up bad management. It is our fault as citizens to let inefficient government happen. The cover-up starts with the local Chamber of Commerce trying not to *rock the boat* knowing quite well that the closure of a facility will be bad for local businesses. It extends to unions afraid to lose members and, therefore, income.

116

The next groups of people to keep this under the table are the congressmen, senators, and governors who are all afraid to lose votes if workers are laid off or the local economy is going to be hurt.

Inefficient government businesses are kept running sometimes without any real purpose (the same can be said of some departments of larger private companies). A case in point: My factory was located not too far from a Navy shipyard, which overhauls (repairs) one, or sometimes, two, nuclear submarines. This Yard used to employ 8,200 full-time plus 800 *part-time* workers. The last element was a ploy by the Yard's management to pull the wool over Congress's eyes. These 800 employees would be hired two months before the budget review process. Then four months later, these employees would be laid off as a sign of good *will* towards Congress (See how efficient we are? We promise to do the same job by saving 10% of the workforce - "applause"). The local papers even advertised in their *help wanted* ads that the positions to be filled were only *part time jobs* and were to last only six months. This ploy worked for many years!

When guests would visit my company, I would sometimes take them to a restaurant located on the river across from the Navy Yard. After pointing out the facilities and explaining their functions, I gave my guests a test of sorts. I asked them to guess how many workers they thought it would take to repair two nuclear submarines, taking into consideration that hardly more than 50 persons could *work* in such tight

117

surroundings without bumping into each other. I also cautioned them to consider that the yard is not a moneymaking enterprise, but a Government-run facility. The answers from the mostly very experienced people (some company presidents themselves) ranged in numbers from 300 to a maximum of 1,200 employees. They were stunned when I told them the true number was 8,200!

With the end of the cold war and the decommissioning of many submarines, the Yard finally has had to make some cutbacks, and the current employment stands around 3,800 (for a while there was not a single submarine in the Yard). So aside from paying all these people for political or social reasons, what do all of these people do? The answer may surprise you. They are all very busy!

Here is a breakdown of the various major departments and the labor as of 1996:

Department	Number of Employees
Engineers (quality and process)	296
Administration & Accounting	578
Entertainment	27
Electronic Data System	358
Training and Education	225
Public Relations	53
Machine Shop	278
Power Plants	136
Yard facilities	120
Maintenance	178

(Continued on next page)

(Continued) **Department**	**Number of Employees**
Human Resources	203
Security (other than U.S. Marine guard)	58
Navy Liaison	125
Congressional Liaison	37
Procurement	413
Communication	62
Print Shop	112
Warehousing/Storage	155
Yard workforce (people who actually *perform work* inside a submarine)	<u>395</u>
TOTAL	**3,809**

As you can see, everybody is not only gainfully employed but also very busy with some overtime thrown in to make up for time lost due to vacation and illnesses. This, of course, does not take into account the occasional goof-off who hides in the supply room to read Playboy® Magazine.

Oh yes, you may be surprised, but there really is a department for entertainment, which utilizes its own 650-seat theater! I suppose it's there in case employees get too bored.

Now, I hasten to say that the above organizational chart is entirely the product of my imagination knowing quite well that this type of data is highly classified. The last thing I need is the F.B.I. knocking on my door.

The work you and I may consider non-productive is of very high value to the affected employees. Consider, for example, the three-year study of the Engineering Department on how to increase efficiency at the Yard. The outcome of these many thousands of man-hours was a new procedure whereby a yard worker would look up the drawing for a given piece of equipment and *then* go inside the submarine to take the part out. In the old system, they would go inside the submarine, look at the part, and then go and get the drawing. I kid you not!

Consider the machinist I once hired as a part-time worker. His main job was working the night shift at the Navy Yard were he was assigned to a gear hobbing machine*. Like his counter-part during the day shift, he actually did not perform any work other than stand by *in case* somewhere in the world a propulsion gear would break. A *code red* would be related to the Yard by radio, which would then cause the worker to push the *start* button on his machine and produce a new gear.

Placing a spare gear in the warehouse would do no good. Since gears break very infrequently, chances are that this spare gear would lie on the shelf for more than one year, and under Navy regulations, equipment that is not used within a year is to be discarded. So you see, it makes perfectly good sense to pay people to do nothing!

---

* A machine to cut teeth into a gear used in this case to drive the propeller.

120

It has not always been this way. During World War II, the Yard was one of the most efficient production facilities for diesel-powered submarines. If we go back farther, we find a very dramatic decrease in the ratio between effective and supportive (administrative) personnel. For example, according to a report in the *Army and Navy Chronicle*,[*] dated 8/20/1840, the budget of the French Navy was listed as: 7,539,700 Francs for officers; 19,066,000 Francs for enlisted men, and only 666,500 Francs for administrative personnel, or only 2.4% of the total were administrative personnel expenses!

In his famous book, *Parkinson's Law*,[**] C.N. Parkinson related that in the British Navy dockyards the number of supportive personnel grew from 5.7% of the total in 1914 to 7.3% in 1928--an increase of 28% in 14 years. The trend to increase the *supportive* number of employees seems to have accelerated in more recent times, perhaps due to the demands of increasing communications (after all, in 1914, there was only Morse code, now we have e-mail). Anyhow, Parkinson found that the British staff of the colonial office, for example, increased by an average of 5.89% per year between 1935 and 1954. This was despite the fact that most of the colonies gained independence during this period.

---

[*] *Army and Navy Chronicle*, (Washington, D.C., 1840)
[**] Parkinson, C.N., *Parkinson's Law*, (Boston: Houghton Mifflin Co., 1975)

We, of course have the same problem here in the USA. In a recent Editorial in *USA TODAY,* it was stated that mismanagement in Defense increased the percentage of overhead from 33% to 66% over a period of 15 years. At that rate the overhead percentage will be 83% in another 15 years (around 2015), or only $17 of every $100 appropriated will be used to purchase actual hardware. The rest goes to overhead expenses according to our *Law of the Sphere* employed here to predict the future based on the last 15 years of figures. Any further money allocated by Congress *to fight waste* will do no good since this money will only add another layer of auditors on top of the pile, leading to even higher rate of overhead!

What does this all mean to us as businesspersons? Well, if thousands of people can exist in Government toiling to communicate, teach, support, and otherwise keep each other occupied, then the same can happen, perhaps on a smaller scale, within certain departments of private companies. One type of private industry that comes close to operate like government enterprises is public utilities. Prior to de-regulation it made no difference how efficient you were and how bloated your staff was. The State Utility Commissions would always allow you a rate increase to cover expenses so that a 10% profit was always guaranteed. Alas, this is no longer true and Utilities have to adapt.

Here is an example: A utility company located in Vermont found itself in the red after de-regulation and floundered on the edge of bankruptcy. They had 14 senior executives and 400 employees eating away whatever profit there was. After cutting the dividend and threats by their banks, management finally came to their senses and made drastic cuts in employment. Now there are only 196 employees and 6 senior executives causing the earnings to increase from -1.3% to plus 5% after taxes! Now sales are up to $1.3 million per employee from only $400,000. This again shows that even in private enterprise an amazingly large number of employees are really *not needed* to run the show!

Isn't it remarkable that following massive lay-offs in the U.S. industry during and after the last recession (1992), the profit of most of those companies exploded, which in turn led to one of the biggest bull markets the United States has ever had. Internal vigilance by management and tight control of the budget are needed to avoid such uncontrolled growth in bureaucracy that, like a cancer, can destroy a healthy organization from within.

Don't be fooled by the fact that all employees in a given department are working hard. The only question is: Does their work produce profit? As you can see from the above example of the Navy Yard, the only *effective* employees are those 395 people actually doing the repair work (10.4% of the total). Yet, the Yard would still exist and everybody would still be working eight hours a day if those 395 effective employees were to be laid off! This is the lesson we can draw from such an organization: The size of an organization or department has nothing to do with the stated purpose, or as C.N. Parkinson so eloquently stated: "Work expands to fill the time available."

With government activities tending to expand over the years and the private sector not supplying enough *fuel* in the form of taxes, as it happened in the early 1990s, the *take* by the government from the Gross Domestic Product (GDP) increases percentage wise.

Contrary to the pronouncement of our liberal politicians, such extra spending does *not* increase growth in our overall economy.

An article in the *Wall Street Journal* dated April 10, 1989 based on a study by Professor Gwartney of Florida State University, showed data, which is reproduced in Figure 10-1. The data from various countries show conclusively that if taxes are too high (government spends too much of GDP), then the resultant economical expansion is very meager.

As a matter of fact, the five most rapidly expanding economies in 1995 (Hong Kong, Singapore, South Korea, Taiwan, and Thailand) had only 20% of GDP *taken* by their governments. Highly taxed countries such as the United States or United Kingdom had only a fraction of the rate of growth experienced by the low-taxed countries. It is no accident that the countries with the highest tax rates as a percent of GDP are also much larger in size than those with the smaller tax rates confirming, again, that *smaller is better*.

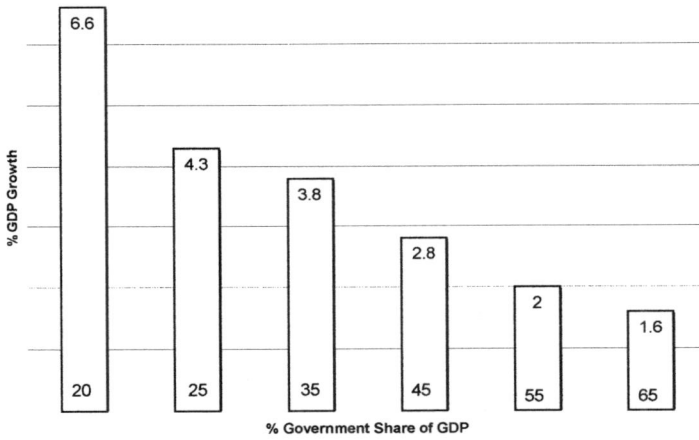

Figure 10-1 Size of government and annual growth of real GDP for OECD countries: 1960 to 1996.

Chapter 11

Why Smaller Is Better

"If it were true that smaller is better, then a flea would be a better animal than an elephant." - A famous writer of management books[*]

From an emotional point of view I certainly agree with the above statement. After all, elephants don't bite me, besides they certainly look much better than a flea. Nevertheless, the flea can outperform the elephant ounce for ounce when it comes to physical power. Why is this, and does the same relationship apply to businesses?

To say smaller companies are more profitable sounds like hearsay in an age that glorifies mergers and big business. Sure, a larger company has more sales and typically more profit than a smaller enterprise. However, what we usually don't see is that the percentage of profit on sales of a larger enterprise is

---

[*] From private correspondence.

126

usually lower than that of a smaller competitor. In other words, smaller enterprises tend to be more efficient than their larger brethren. We may be better able to understand why this is by observing nature. In nature we see distinct differences in metabolism and work performed per given time between smaller and larger animals all following so-called *Scaling Laws*. Such laws define the rate of metabolism per unit of body weight between larger and smaller animals, or the ratio between the surface area and the volume of a sphere, for example. The question is, could such scaling laws apply to businesses?

For modeling purposes, one could consider, for example, that like the surface area of a sphere, the number of *effective,* i.e. profit-producing employees increases only to the square of the diameter, while the total number of employees, much like the volume of a sphere, increases to the cube of the diameter, as I will explain later.

Hence, the larger the company gets, the smaller the number of *effective,* i.e., profit-contributing employees compared to the over all employment. As a result, the rate of profit decreases.

Scaling factors in nature

Just as Adam Smith's *invisible hand* regulates markets, so perhaps do the equivalent of natural scaling factors affect the profitability of businesses. Can it be that bigger is not necessarily better? All

127

companies want to grow, a quite healthy thing to do, but are we going about this growth in the most profitable way?

Scaling laws in nature regulate certain physical phenomena and behavior. Some of us have experienced dust storms driven by 40 to 50 miles per hour winds. Luckily for us the sand particles we feel are rather small, averaging less than five one-hundredths (0.05) of an inch in diameter. Larger stones, say one half-inch (0.5) in diameter, stay on the ground. The reason is that the stones obey the 2/3rd power scaling factor or "*The Principle of Similitude*", as D'Arcy Thompson formulated in 1917 in *On Growth and Form.*

Quoting Thompson: "*it often happens that of the forces in action in a system some vary as one power and some as another, of the ...magnitudes involved.*" Thus, returning to our sand pebble example, a one-half inch diameter stone weighs one *thousand* times more than the average grain of sand since the volume and weight vary to the third power. However, the same stone exposes just a one *hundred* times greater surface area to the wind than the grain of sand, since surface area varies only to the second power. Hence, the larger stone has only 10% of the surface area per ounce than the smaller one. The wind pressure must therefore increase 10 times to lift the larger stone!

Scaling factors affect the animal kingdom also. A smaller animal has proportionally more surface area than a larger one, approximating the ¾ power-scaling factor. More surface area means that more thermal energy is radiated away from the surface of the animal allowing for more work to be done in the form of muscle movement in a given time period. The transfer of heat through the radiation of thermal energy results from a temperature differential that provides the thermodynamic potential for work. The more efficiently heat is continuously radiated the more power can be produced. A smaller body with a larger surface area does this more efficiently.

People experience this power-scale relationship whenever we work in the tropics where we find that our *rate of work* slows down considerably without benefit of air conditioning. This means that we still can dig a ditch (same work), but it takes us perhaps twice as long as up north (we perform only *one half* the power).

The reason is that while we have an unchanged surface area, the temperature difference is less between our body temperature and that of the surrounding air. Hence, less thermal energy can be radiated and, therefore, less muscle power is produced. We would notice the same effect if our body surface somehow would be less. This is exactly what happens to obese people even in moderate climates. On the opposite side, a very lean person has relatively more radiating body surface and, therefore, can produce more power per ounce of body weight, as photographs of the winners of the Boston Marathon illustrate. (I hope you will forgive me for this not quite politically correct comparison).

129

Take another example: A mouse weighs about 1 ounce (0.0625 pounds) while a man may weigh 160 pounds. Assuming a 3/4 power scaling factor, the surface area and thereby the metabolic rate, or food intake of the mouse, is about 7 times greater than that of a human per ounce of body weight. D'Arcy Thompson and others have shown that the absolute work output per ounce of body weight of all animals is roughly the same. It follows from the simplest definition of work (weight times distance) that, say, a flea, a man, or an elephant jumping seven inches straight up (a feat of which each is capable) are producing about the same work *per unit weight*.

Here is the question: If the work done is the same, why then is the power output of smaller animals higher? Why is the metabolic rate higher for smaller mammals than larger ones? The answer is they can perform *the same amount of work much faster*. Power is, after all, defined as work per unit time. Calories are converted into power, or work per second. In theory, 192,000 mice (the same weight as one elephant) could move given objects in one second while it would take the elephant 20 seconds to do the same![*]

In another example, an elephant can carry a log weighing no more than 1,100 pounds. Now 15 men can carry the same log (about 70 pounds for each) the same distance and in the same time as an elephant does. Yet it would take 70 men to equal the weight of

---

[*] Using a ¾ power scaling factor (see following pages).

130

an average elephant. This shows that *man*, a smaller *animal* than the elephant, is on average 470% more power efficient.

Scaling factors and business

Since such scaling factors can be shown to apply to mice and elephants, could it not be that, as with animals, a smaller, homogenous manufacturing enterprise could be more power efficient, producing more widgets in a given time period than its larger counterpart?

Scaling Laws, when applied to businesses, means that *profit does not increase in linear proportion to sales growth or,* for that matter, *business size, but rather at a lesser, exponential rate.* This rate is defined by a <u>power-scaling factor</u>.

Using the ¾ power scaling factor, we could postulate that a given company with 100 people could produce the same number of *widgets* per employee as a competitor with 1,000 employees but $1,000/100$ x $(100/1,000)^{3/4}$ = 1.78 times faster. Expressed differently, 6 plants of the smaller variety could produce the same number of widgets per month as a single plant 10 times as big. The reason for this is that in the larger plant more people work in jobs unrelated to the actual production of widgets, since each of the actual production workers in the large, as well as in the smaller plants, can produce the same amount of widgets in a given time period. Expressed differently, the larger plants have more overhead. If this is true, then smaller, homogeneous enterprises (single profit centers with their own management and accounting systems but without any sub-divisions or subsidiaries) will be more profitable.

For our purposes, scaling laws may be usefully employed as a model to help predict certain maximum size relationships within manufacturing entities. It certainly will not prevent an incompetent manager of a small firm from having a dismal profit picture. On the other side of the coin, a large enterprise may have an exceptionally large profit due to its quasi-monopoly in a given business. Such cases should be excluded from this analysis.

Figure 11-1 shows a typical relationship. Here I plotted the pre-tax earnings in percent of sales against the annual sales volume of manufacturing companies, which are essentially in the same, or closely related market and are either homogeneous organizations or independent divisions of larger firms. The reference values shown for the calculations were arbitrarily chosen to match the $10 million sales point at 35 % profit. A 2/3rd power factor is used.

Figure 11-1

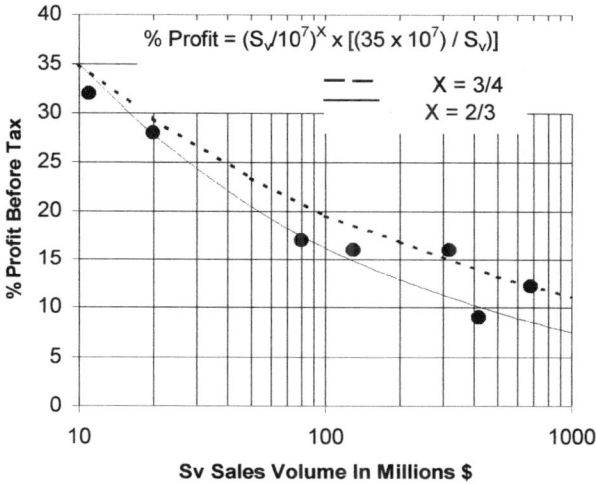

% Profit = $(S_v/10^7)^X \times [(35 \times 10^7)/S_v)]$

X = 3/4
X = 2/3

Sv Sales Volume In Millions $

In a January 12, 1999 *New York Times* article entitled, "Of Mice and Elephants; A matter of Scale," it was stated that Kleiber, in the 1930's, found that metabolic rate scales with body mass not with the originally assumed 2/3-rd power but closer to the 3/4 power. I, therefore, superimposed a curve following the ¾-power scale on to Figure 11-1. The data points fall somewhere in between. Nevertheless either scaling factor clearly shows a trend away from greater efficiency when a homogenous enterprise or, for that matter, a conglomerate with equally growing divisions, expands.

Why then do larger corporations exist and even make a decent rate of profit? The answer is because they are never a homogenous organization (i.e., one factory under one roof) but a conglomerate of a number of semi-independent organizations each with its own profit and sales numbers. This is much like pearls on a string (see Figure 11-2). If such companies grow mostly through acquisition or mergers, then their average rate of profit on sales will remain about the same.

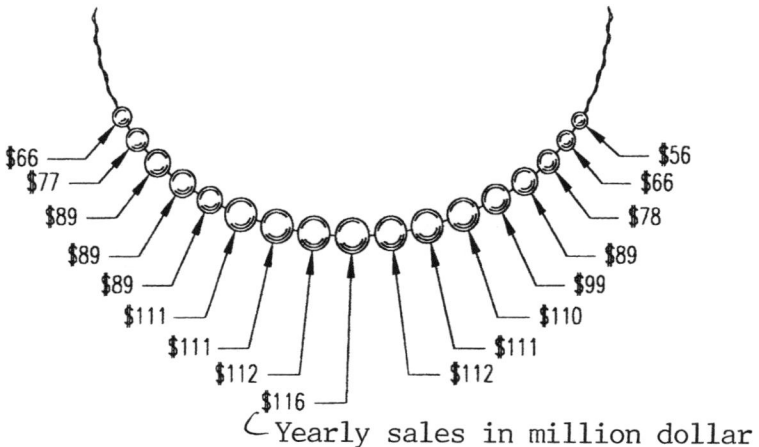

$66
$77
$89
$89
$89
$111
$111
$112
$116

$56
$66
$78
$89
$99
$110
$111
$112

Yearly sales in million dollar

Figure 11-2 Schematic depiction of conglomerate with 17 separate divisions

For example, Figure 11-2 shows 17 individual divisions with a total yearly sales volume of $1.581 billion with a total average profit of 11.5%. If this corporation were to add one more division having a sales volume of $120 million with a profit rate of 14%, then the overall average profit rate will be 11.7%, or hardly a change at all. Clearly, no scaling factors apply here unless each division grows by itself. Nevertheless, even multi-divisional companies can experience slow erosion of their pre-tax profit due to the scaling effects in their growing divisions. An example of such a case is shown in Figure 11-3. Here the *after tax* earnings of a well-run U.S.-based corporation is plotted showing a rather impressive growth over the years.

However, if the earnings *before tax* are plotted in Figure 11-4, we see a slow but gradual erosion. The reason is that the effective tax rate of this company decreased from 44% to 36% over the given period, thereby, masking the actual reduction in operating efficiency and the resultant pre-tax earning decrease.

The gradual erosion of profit can also be seen when over all employment increases. In Figure 11-5, I plotted total employment and pre-tax profit for automobile companies and their suppliers to illustrate this point. All companies are listed on U.S. stock exchanges and include General Motors (the largest employer), Ford, and even Volvo, for example. On the smaller employment scale are parts suppliers. This is a fair comparison since all these companies are essentially in the same business and undergo similar competitive and labor related pressures. The dotted line is the predicted trend of all data points using the

¾ scaling law (assuming 20% profit for 1,000 employees as an arbitrary starting point.)

Although there is a lack of input on the low side, the available data shows an unmistakable trend towards lower profit numbers with increase in employment despite the fact that the larger corporations do employ quite a number of financially independent divisions. However, in my opinion, there should have been even more independent divisions in order to improve profit.

Earnings of Major Equipment Manufacturer
1983 - 1998

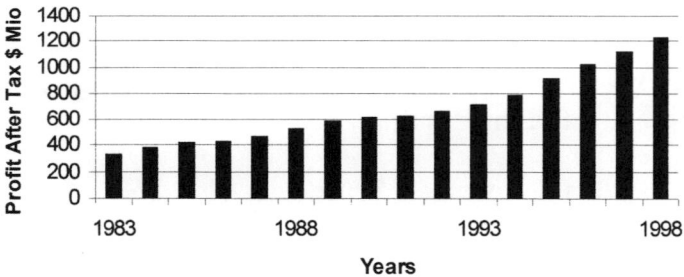

Figure 11-3

% Earnings of Major Equipment Manufacturer
1983 - 1998

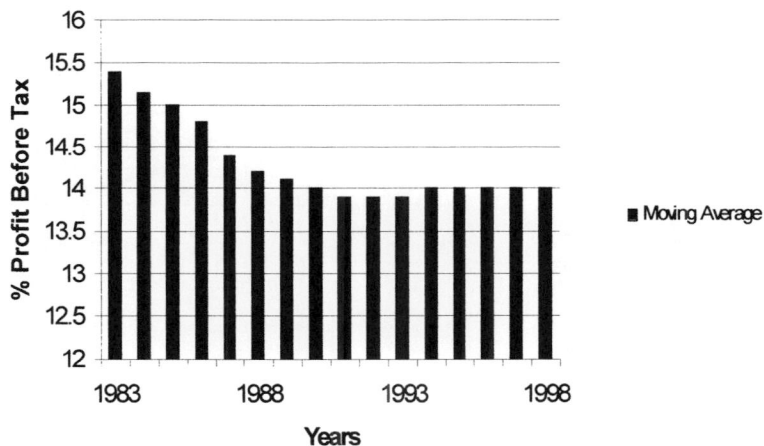

Figure 11-4

Tax rates: 1993= 43.9%; 1998= 36.1%
Difference between pre-, and after tax rate showing hidden loss of efficiency.

**Relationship Between Number of Employees and Profit Before Income Tax in the
Automotive and Automotive Parts Industries
(Source: Value Line Investment Survey^R, 1999)**

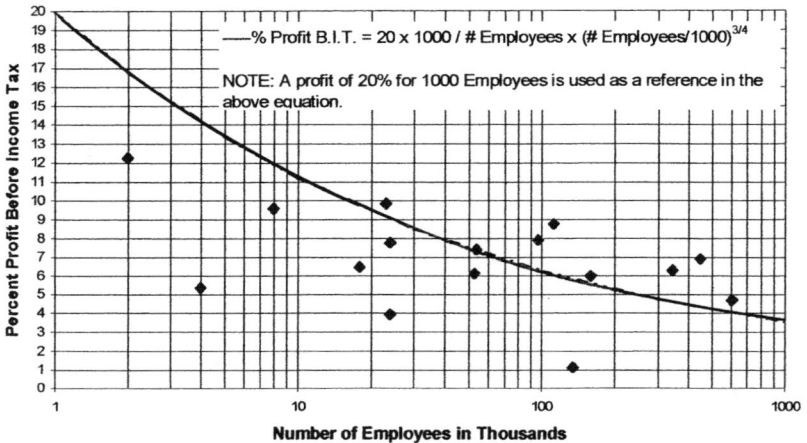

$$\text{% Profit B.I.T.} = 20 \times 1000 \,/\, \text{# Employees} \times (\text{# Employees}/1000)^{3/4}$$

NOTE: A profit of 20% for 1000 Employees is used as a reference in the above equation.

Percent Profit Before Income Tax

Number of Employees in Thousands

Figure 11-5

Why is this happening?

Is there is a correlation between company sales volume and profit or, similarly, between sales volume and number of employees? Is there a connection between the number of employees and profit before tax? What is the real reason?

One simple explanation is that as a company grows, its number of *effective* or profit-producing employees could vary as the second power of the relative size of the company while the number of *total* employees may vary as the third power of the size. This mimics the relationship between the surface area and the volume of a sphere; hence *Law of the Sphere* (see

138

Chapter 12). Mind you, the efficiency of the *individual* production worker in either the small or the larger plant is roughly the same. Where the inefficiency comes in is that the production worker in the larger plant has to support many more of the non-effective employees (staff, etc.) than is the case in the smaller factory.

An organization chart can illustrate how efficiency and profitability can degenerate with the growth of companies. Let's start with an Example: A single individual starts an enterprise with three production workers. His organization is shown in Figure 11-6A. Here the ratio between production workers and overall employment is an impressive $3/4 = 0.750$. Let' call it 75% efficient.

After some growth, our man hires three foremen and six additional production workers (see Figure 11-6B) maintaining the same 3:1 worker to boss relationship.

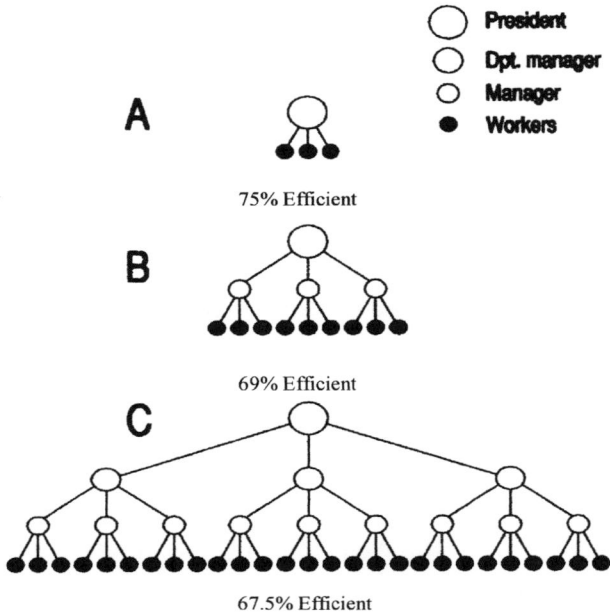

A

75% Efficient

B

69% Efficient

C

67.5% Efficient

Figure 11-6 Simple Organization chart of company with 3 reporting levels.

However, now the ratio between production and total employment decreased to $9/13 = 0.692$, or about 69% efficient.

Growing even further, his total employment swells to 40. Yet with still the same worker to boss relationship, his efficiency decreased further to $27/40 = 67\%$ as seen in Figure 11-6C.

What we have seen so far are very lean organizations with no fat. But let's assume our president in Figure 11-6B wants to add a secretary and a file clerk onto his staff... quite a reasonable request. After all, with growth he can no longer handle all the paperwork himself. Doing this brings the overall employment from 13 to 15 persons, which decreases our ratio from 0.692 to 9/15 = 0.600 as shown in Figure 11-7B-1. Now we lost 9% efficiency!

Later on he needs to expand his staff even further, commensurate with his increase in business. He adds six staff people in addition to hiring 18 production workers. This certainly sounds fair, does it not? However, as Figure 11-7C-1 now shows, his ratio between production workers and overall employees is now down to 27/48 = 0.563, i.e. his plant efficiency went down to 56%!

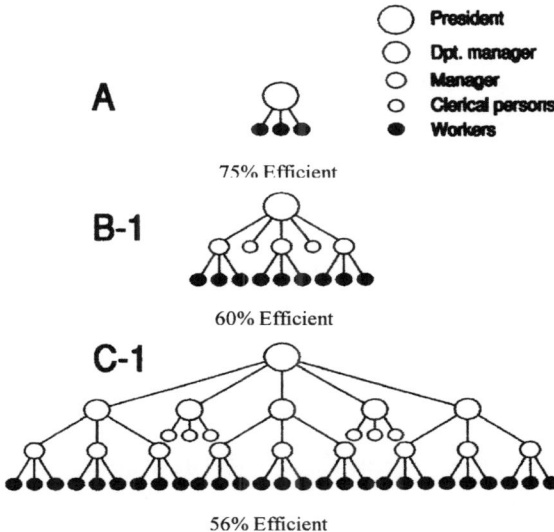

Figure 11-7 Organization chart of company with added clerical help.

What does this all mean to our budding entrepreneur? First the good news. Growing from four employees (including himself) to 48 increased his sales volume by 100 x 27/3 = 900%. Now the bad news. His profit grew by only 100 x (56 x 27)/(75 x 3) = 672%. Lowering his overall plant efficiency cost him 25% of profit potential!

This is the reality encountered by growing companies. It is nearly impossible to keep growing and yet maintain the same ratio between production workers and overall employment that a desired constant operating efficiency (% profit on sales) demands.

The above example also gives a good explanation of how the *invisible Law of the Sphere* operates: *Total employment grows at a higher exponential rate than the rate of growth of production workers (*"effective" employees).

For the mathematically inclined, the ratio between the *effective* and the *total* number of employees in a company can be stated using the symbol N for the number of workers reporting to each manager (it is assumed that this number remains constant throughout the organization, i.e., at all layers of the hierarchy), and that L designates the number of reporting levels in the organization (including the president). Then the *efficiency* ratio, that is the ratio between production worker and overall employees is:

$$\text{Ratio} = N^L / 1 + N + N^2 + \ldots + N^L$$

For example: Assuming there are 6 workers per each manager ($N = 6$) and there are 3 reporting levels ($L = 3$) then the

Ratio $= N^3 / 1 + N + N^2 + N^3 = 0.834$, or restated

Ratio $= N^3 / N^3 + N^2 + N + 1$.

Now the right hand side of the equation has the characteristic of a *cubic equation*. It shows that the number of total employees (right side of the fraction) increases at a faster rate than the number of effective *or productive* employees (numerator, or left-hand side of the fraction).

But like a cubic equation, the rate of decrease in the *ratio* is diminishing with increase in the number of reporting levels. The biggest decrease in the *ratio,* i.e., decrease in efficiency occurs between the 1st and the 4th reporting level. Little changes occur thereafter. This, however, does not include the detrimental effects of adding clerical workers and additional staff layers to the organization (see Figure 11-7). Here the efficiency ratio decreases much faster and at a less predictable rate.

A second reason, and related to the above, may be that there are too many layers of management when organizations grow. These unnecessary layers can place a burden on support services like the burden placed on the heart of an obese animal, which must pump significantly more blood to more tissue without any real increase in heart capacity. It also severely restricts the communication flow from the decision-making top to the executing lower layers of the organization.

If we wanted to limit the number of management layers to five and assuming an average number of eight persons per department, the total number of employees of such a company could not exceed 645 persons! This is hardly a mid-size plant.

The mathematical relationship described here implies that further growth of such an enterprise under one roof would then require additional layers of management. The detrimental effects of excessive management layers are widely known and commented on by Tom Peters, for example.

Third, is the decreasing effectiveness of communication with size? The increasing number of departments may lead to an increasing number of decision makers on various levels within the hierarchy which in turn produces invariable delays in, and watering down of, vital and, perhaps worse, even mundane business decisions.

Fourth, there invariably appears a proliferation of non-profit contributing departments, which while seemingly necessary, such as Environmental and Loss Prevention, nevertheless, suck out vital company resources and manpower.

Fifth, business enterprise computer software gets exceedingly complex with larger organizations, and the cost of ownership soars.

Smaller businesses have organizational structures that offer a certain *transparency* that gets lost. For example, the owner of a small auto repair shop with 25 employees knows quite well how his company is organized and what everybody is supposed to do. On the other hand, even department managers in firms with several thousands of employees, let alone the CEOs of such firms, are at a loss to understand or explain their *enterprise system.*

Finally, with growth we see a disappearance of the original entrepreneurial spirit and with it the *esprit du corps* or enthusiasm of the employees. It is easy to see that even major department managers in large firms spend more time maintaining the status quo or worry about their own security than about their customers or their company's profitability. While this can partially be countered with a proper profit-sharing plan (see INCENTIVES), the way to distribute such incentives in a fair and equitable way becomes more difficult in larger firms.

After reading the above, the reader may wonder if I am ignoring the obvious benefits of large organizations, which are typically conglomerates? The truth is they are partly myths. A conglomerate's combined purchasing power, which is often cited as a benefit, can be a detriment since it forces the divisions into the hands of a few *monopoly* suppliers with no

145

competitive bidding and vulnerability to strikes. As another example, a corporate-wide R&D department cannot possibly understand the technical complexity of each division's products. Even legal support services should be subject to competitive bidding by local law offices.

Consider this example of a conglomerate's *cost-saving* idea: A corporate headquarters, located in a major city, made a nation-wide deal with a local travel agent to supply airline tickets to all of their divisions. In return, the agent would pay back 5% of all fares to the corporation. The trouble was that the city where the headquarters was located was the hub of one larger airline, which, due to its near monopoly, charged excessive fares. Needless to say, the local agent favored this carrier due to higher commissions and so did the corporate headquarters since it received 5% of all. The sufferers in all of this, besides the shareholders, were the CEOs of the divisions since they were saddled with a 15% to 20% higher travel budget.

Lessons to be learned

What can we learn from all of this? If we accept that smaller is better then we can devise a strategy around this concept. First, in the case of a rapidly growing company, make every effort to split it by product lines into two smaller, financially independent parts. The key to success, as always, is to find competent and trained general managers. Do not, at your peril, put managers in charge who have been trained in a very large facility.

If you expand by acquisition, then leave the newly acquired organization alone unless the management was really bad. The corporate CEO of the parent company should make it his or her highest priority to avoid unnecessary interference by corporate staff people in the operation of divisions.

Scaling down the size of the parent staff headquarters will always be a good remedy for such problems. The same philosophy applies to mergers. Try to keep production, marketing, and even the Logo of each merger partners intact as much as possible. The ultimate aim of all your actions as CEO should be to maintain, if not grow, the *rate of profit*, that is the percentage of profit on sales, while your business is growing.

As Meadows, et al. stated in their book *Beyond the Limits*, our industrial production is still highly inefficient. Let's start by devising more efficient company operating structures.

We already see this trend towards smaller and more efficient manufacturing plants. Mini steel mills replacing their non-profitable larger predecessors come to mind. As the *ECONOMIST* in their February 13, 1999, issue stated: "The future lies with smaller, and more flexible factories, like the ones General Motors is building in Brazil and Michigan".

147

Like steel mills and auto plants, other factories will follow, forced by competitive pressure to reduce primarily overhead and stay, or become again, more profitable.

One final consideration, it is better if a single division fails, be it due to mismanagement, litigation, or, product obsolescence than bestowing such a problem on to a single, large firm. The negative financial impact for the large firm is greater by far than even the complete loss of a small division.

Chapter 12

Law Of The Sphere

Increases in manufacturing efficiency barely keep up with the increase in administrative expenses.

To paraphrase the old saying: "If you are not a liberal under 30, you have no heart; if you are not a conservative over 40, you have no brain." I like to propose: "If you don't believe in a centralized corporate structure under 30, you flunked your MBA exams; if you don't believe in a decentralized organization by the time you are 40, then don't start a business!"

There are, off course, exceptions. For example, a shipyard needing thousands of people under one roof to build a nuclear air craft carrier can hardly be split into separate profit centers. But these should stay exceptions and should not distract from our aim to manage with more and smaller individual profit centers instead of larger and more cumbersome single corporate enterprises.

While never having attended a business school, I nevertheless was enthralled by the seemingly obvious economics of large combined corporate structures when I was a young man. After all, a large corporation has more corporate resources and a well-staffed R&D Department that a small company never could afford, not to mention the big clout of the corporate marketing and sales staff. In addition, you have the centralized purchasing power to put all kinds of cost cutting pressure on your vendors.

When I got older and had practical exposure to the ways smaller and larger companies worked, I found that similar to large central governments, any technical efficiency achieved by greater size were eaten away by the *human factor*. By *human factor* I mean the resultant impersonalization of the individual employee, the stifling inefficiencies of multi-layered management, and worst of all, by the constant attempts by middle management to accumulate staff and to build empires.

When debating the issue of small vs. large companies, one must distinguish between two categories of employees.

1. The *effective* employee
2. The *supportive* employee

Note that I use the term *effective* instead of *efficient*. To make my point, a manager working in the Environmental Service Department of a large corporation might be very efficient in writing letters to the Federal Government outlining plans to avoid spills, but this effort is not effective in increasing sales and, therefore, profit (this does not imply the job is not necessary. After all, a fine by the government can be costly and cause bad public relations!).

For the purpose of this study, I will categorize those employees whose work is not directly related to sales and production as *supportive*. This category would include employees in departments such as Research and Development, Marketing, Public Relations, Human Resources, stockholder relations, and others of this sort.

In his book, *The Dilbert Principle,*[*] Scott Adams defines *non-fundamental work* (done by supportive staff) as:

Quality fair	Employee satisfaction survey
Process improvement team	Suggestion system
Recognition committee	ISO9000
Standards	Reorganization
Policy improvement	Budget process
Writing vision statements	Writing an *approved*
Writing mission statements	*equipment list*

---

[*] Adams, Scott, *The Dilbert Principle*, (Harper Collins), 1996.

He further defined *non-fundamental work* as: "any activity that is one level removed from your people or your product."

In looking at the above table, most sensible people would readily agree that the majority of the stated activities are not necessary and usually the result of popular fads. However, the larger the company, the more unnecessary activities are tolerated.

It is difficult to measure the output of employees who work in supportive departments, which is usually related to the effectiveness of their supervisor. Such effectiveness is impaired if (1) there is not enough backup work (not knowing what to do when my current work assignment is completed will produce *rubber work*, or, again, in the words of C.N. Parkinson[*]: "Work expands to fill the time available," and (2) if the supervisor does not have the technical background to understand the work he assigns (he is at the mercy of his staff and has to believe in all real or imaginary problems that a given project encounters).

Strictly considering the direct impact on the business performance of a company, *effective* employees are personnel involved in direct sales support, production, including direct production supervision, planning and purchasing (strictly related to business inventories), and engineering personnel involved in order related

---

[*] Parkinson, C. Northote, *Parkinson's Law*, (Boston: Houghton Mifflin Co.), 1975.

efforts. In other words, an *effective* employee is any person whose effort leads directly to obtaining and executing a customer order and whose effort, therefore, has a direct impact on the profitability of the enterprise.

As you can see, my examples are related to manufacturing companies where the distinction can most readily be made. (However, a similar analysis should apply to other businesses as well.)

A good manager is interested in having a high ratio of *effective* to *supportive* employees in his company, or a high E/S ratio. Achieving this is your ticket to profitability. I strongly believe that control of the E/S ratio is the most important task of any chief executive officer. Growth in the *effective* category is usually business related. If order volume increases, you first work overtime and later hire more personnel. This is a relatively easy task and the whole process is nearly transparent. On the other hand, when orders decrease, such as in a recession, you reverse the process. First, you reduce working hours, and then you terminate positions. Unfortunately, the latter typically does not happen in the *supportive* category. Terminating supportive positions usually is an act of desperation, i.e., when times are tough and the balance sheet is awash in red ink. Why is this true? Well one of the reasons is that staff positions tend to become *invisible* compared to hourly wages and widgets produced per hour. There are endless business studies on how to improve *efficiencies* in production, but hardly any on how to improve efficiencies of staff people. How does one measure the efficiency of a marketing person? If it took ten people to come up with a brand name for a *new and improved* detergent, could five persons do just as well? Probably.

In my past association with medium-sized manufacturing companies, I was absolutely astonished to see management hire consultants to time study the performance of the machine shop to determine the machining time of individual parts expressed in minutes to the fourth decimal place!

This was done even though the union workers made a point of slowing down the normal machine tool speed upon spotting such a timekeeper.

We have this tremendous fascination to reduce direct labor (typically 18% of the selling price) by 5% or 10%, but we think nothing of increasing General and Administrative (G&A) expenses by 2% (hiring time keepers, increase planning staff, etc.) in order to do this. Incidentally, a 10% decrease in direct labor increases profit by about 1.8% while a 10% increase in G&A typically *decreases* profit by 2.7%.

The latest trend in *reducing cost* is to relocate machining facilities from the United States to other countries such as Mexico, Eastern Europe, and Asia. The reason is most managers are fascinated by the direct wage differential, i.e., $15 per hour in Nebraska versus $3.00 per hour in Mexico. This is a very superficial comparison. Since practically all modern tool machines are numerically controlled, their cost is rather high (several hundred thousand dollars each); therefore, the cost of the machine alone is typically $40.00 per hour due to depreciation of the purchase price alone. The real comparison between Mexico and the U.S. is, therefore, $40 + $3 versus $40 + $15, or a 22% cost saving instead of 80%...still not too bad. However, to that you have to add the cost of building a new plant, training your employees (a typically high turnover in Mexico), relocating U.S. supervisors (at higher salaries), increased transportation costs, and such mundane items such as finding trained mechanics to service the electronics. Relocating assembly operations, requiring essentially low cost manual labor with fewer expensive machine tools, makes much more sense. Nevertheless, all these relocation studies consume an awful lot of staff work and travel expenses. *Supportive* cost that is typically not accounted for in the *cost cutting* planning stage!

Returning to the problem of maintaining a decent ratio of effective to *supportive* personnel. One of the biggest problems a CEO faces is determining the optimum, or better yet, the *absolute minimum* number of staff or supportive personnel needed in the organization. This is a daunting task and gets more difficult the larger a company is, i.e., the organizational structure becomes less and less *transparent* with an increase in size. Relying on your department heads in this matter is usually futile. Typical statements will be, "We are already cut to the bone." "We even had more employees during the '82 depression," or "Our Marketing Department is smaller than competitor X. If we reduce our staff further, we will not be able to introduce new products," etc.

The trend in electronic communications will also tend to increase staff requirements. After all, somebody has to read all the extra reports that computers generate. All this is a clear argument for decentralization and smaller-sized companies. Remind yourself that small is beautiful and small is profitable. If nothing else, it restores the transparency of a company's organizational structure to the eyes of the CEO.

Consider the chart in Figure 12-1. It contains plotted performance data for metal fabricating and machining industries taken from *Value Line®*[*] for the year 1994. I excluded companies with sales over $1 billion since those companies are typically conglomerates of many smaller, quasi-independent companies and, therefore, would not be representative for this study. On the other hand, companies below $100 million in annual sales volume were not listed and, therefore, are not included.

The graph demonstrates two things: First, it is amazing how many companies are satisfied with a profit B.I.T. of only 5% to 10%. Apparently their measure of success is to be comparable to their competitors. Second, this chart shows a definite trend towards higher profit with decreasing sales, i.e., smaller company size. For example, the average

---

[*] *Value Line®*, Value Line Publishing Inc., 1994.

profit for companies with between $500 million and $1,000 million in sales is 6.17%, for those between $250 and $500 million it's 8.4%, and between $100 to $250 million it's 11.6%!

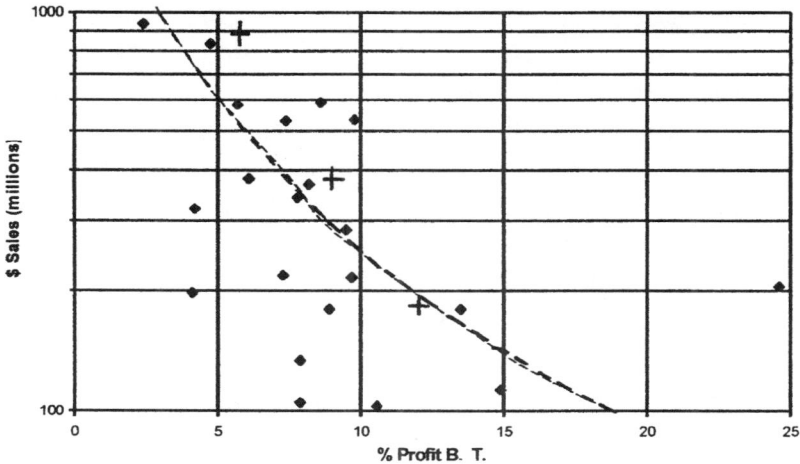

FIGURE 12-1 Relationship between sales and earnings before tax of small- to medium-sized companies (Source: ValueLine®, 1994 data) + = Average values ----- = Calculated values where % profit = $4(1000/Sales)^{2/3}$

One of the problems encountered with larger sized companies is the number of layers of management In his excellent book, *Thriving in Chaos*[*], Tom Peters suggests limiting the number of management layers to no more than five, with between 25 to 75 people

---

[*] Peters, Thomas, *Thriving in Chaos*, (New York: A. Knopf), 1987

reporting to a manager. Except for manufacturing or purely clerical jobs, (such as data entry in an insurance company), I personally consider more than 25 persons to be non-manageable for one manager.

Let's consider an industrial company and forget the Manufacturing Department, which is usually not the problem in any organization. There are typically ten departments such as Sales, Marketing, Order Entry, Engineering, Research and Development, Human Resources, Purchasing, Planning, Accounting, and Customer Service. Assuming each is staffed with 25 persons, there would be 250 plus 10 managers equaling 260 employees, not including the CEO. This would be a three-layer company. If the company is larger, we find 25 sub-sections in each of the ten major departments of 25 people each.

This would bring the company up to four management layers and the head count (not adding the manufacturing labor) to $\{[(25 + 1) \times 25] + 25\} \times 10 + 10$ department heads and 1 CEO = 6,761 employees. After adding the CEO, this would be the absolute largest company with a five-layer structure.

However, the reality is that there are typically only four to twelve persons reporting to one supervisor or manager. Using an average size of eight per department and with a maximum layer of five management levels, we have to limit the size of the non-manufacturing portion of any company to only $\{[(8 + 1) \times 8] + 8\} \times 8 + 8$ and 1 CEO = 649 employees! There are then only two ways to increase the company's size: (1) Increase the number of layers of management, or (2) split the company into several smaller, *autonomous*, divisions, i.e., the division should operate all but in name as a completely separate company unfettered by the corporate staff!

Emerson Electric Corporation is one of those companies that successfully kept their divisions independent. The financial results reflect the success of this effort. As their 1996 earning statement proves, with $11,150 million in sales, they achieved a respectable 14.4% profit before taxes, which referring to Figure 12-1, would place them somewhere in the earning range of a single company with about $150 million sales volume.

The implied relationship between company size and profit extends also to separate divisions or different manufacturing facilities of larger enterprises. As stated in previous examples, there is plenty of evidence that smaller divisions typically out perform the larger divisions within the same firm when it comes to percentage of profit on sales.

To call for smaller, leaner organizations is, of course, nothing new. In his book, *Organization and Management in Industry and Business*,[*] originally published in 1928, William B. Cornell (incidentally, a fellow mechanical engineer) argued for centralized executive control even in small firms, which

---

[*] Cornell, William B., *Organization and Management in Industry and Business*, (New York: The Ronald Press Company), 1928.

inadvertently limits the size of the organization; thus, becoming more controllable. If nothing else, it reduces the management by committee syndrome.

There are exceptions, of course. For example, the Catholic Church hierarchy manages 407,750 priests worldwide[*] with only five management layers. Then again, they have had nearly 2000 years of practice. Nevertheless, as Hammer and Champy[**] explain, when you need eleven people to produce 100 widgets a day, you need 193 people (instead of 110) in order to produce 1,000 widgets due to the added support staff. Consider the United States Navy. A typical aircraft carrier needs 5,000 personnel to bring 80 aircraft into action, in other words, it needs more than 60 support people per plane.

An example of how a reduction in layers of management will increase efficiency is given by Tichy and Sherman[***] who reported that General Electric's Lighting Division reduced its layers of management from seven to four with a resultant increase of sales per salaried employee of 35%!

Considering all that, wouldn't it be nice to have a mathematical tool to predict the relationship between size and profitability? A method that would predict

---

[*] *Welt Am Sonntag*, (Germany: Hamburg), Feb. 23, 1997.
[**] Hammer and Champy, *Reengineering the Corporation*, (New York: Harper Business), 1996.
[***] Tichy and Sherman, *Control Your Destiny or Someone Else Will*, (Harper Collins), 1995.

the decrease in profit level when increasing the size of an organization?

Microorganisms found out that smaller is better. Cells, like bacteria, are incredibly small creatures. Evolution, despite all the other changes that have taken place over the millennia, has kept them that small. The reason is that they basically constitute a sphere. The core of the sphere contains just the basic elements for survival and procreation. No extra frills, yet they need a large surface area to interact with other cells or substances. A small diameter gives you that advantage. You lose this advantage the larger the sphere gets.

Consider if you will the two spheres in Figures 12-2. The smaller one has a radius of 1-inch while the larger sphere has a radius of 2 inches. The equations governing the surface area of a sphere, A, and the volumes of a sphere, V, are given as follows:

$$A = 4 \times \pi \times R^2 \text{, or } A = 12.56\,R^2$$
$$V = 4/3 \times \pi \times R^3 \text{, or } V = 4.19\,R^3$$

These equations show that the volume, or the contents of the interior of the sphere, increases to the third power of the radius R. It does this at a much faster rate than the increase in the surface area A of a sphere, which only increases to the square of the radius R. The volume of the sphere with a 2-inch radius is eight times larger than that of the 1-inch radius sphere. Yet the area increased only four times when increasing the radius from a 1-inch to a 2-inch.

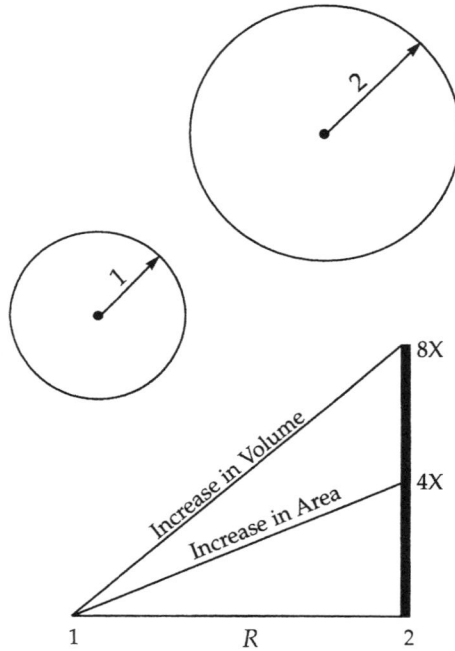

Figure 12-2 Relationship between size, volume, and surface area of differently sized spheres.

Another example is shown in Figure 12-3. At a radius of ½ inch (diameter of 1 inch), for example, the volume happens to be about 0.52 cubic inches and the surface area is 3.14 square inches (a ratio of about 6:1). At 5-inch radius (10-inch diameter), the volume increased to 524 cubic inches while the surface area only increased to $314in^2$ (now the ratio is only 0.6:1). This proves that the volume (after increasing the radius ten times) increased 1,000 times while the surface area only increased 100 times! No wonder bacteria want to stay small! They need a relatively large surface area to interact with adjacent cells still utilizing a minimum core (support structure). The natural limit in the size of a bacterium is governed by the ability of the surface area to feed the core substance (the volume).

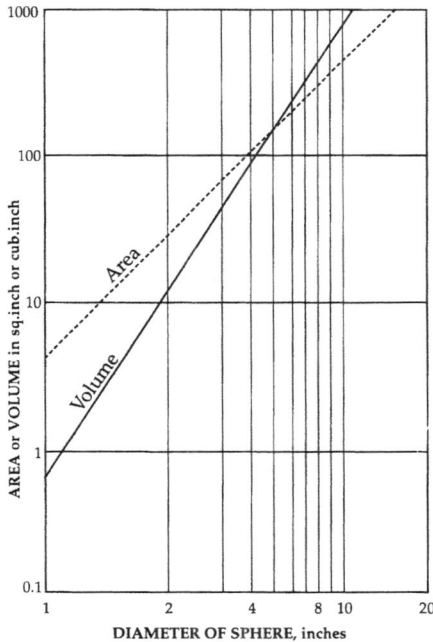

Figure 12-3 Example of how the rate of change between the volume and surface diverges.

163

The previous examples show that the relationship between area increase and volume increase is given by $R^{2/3}$, or what I call the "Law of the Sphere."

What I suspect is that human organizations are also subject to this Law of the Sphere. We may compare the surface area of a sphere to that part of an organization that is actively involved in creating profit such as the external sales force engaging the customer if you are a sales organization, or if the organization is an army, engaging the enemy. In manufacturing, the surface area would include: order fulfillment, direct production labor, and so on. In other words, what I previously defined as an effective labor force.

The volume of the sphere, on the other hand, would comprise the total number of employees, including the previously identified *supportive* personnel. In private industry, this would be Corporate Headquarters, Marketing, R&D, stockholder relations, etc., in addition to Manufacturing and Sales. In the army, this would include staff and logistics, for example. Same as bacteria, a good CEO wants a surface area as large as possible compared to the unavoidable volume. This, of course, predicates a small sphere (small organization).

Does such a *Law of the Sphere*, which tells us that the surface area only increases to the two-thirds power of the volume increase, really apply to human organizations? If so, then it would follow that the effective number of employees E_1 out of a given

164

number of total employees T_1 would increase to a new number of effective employees, E_2, by the two-thirds power of the ratio between the total new number of employees T_2 to the old number T_1, or $E_2 = E_1(T_2 / T_1)^{2/3}$. In analyzing data accumulated from private sources and from business publications, I found that such a relationship exists, which while not as mathematically perfect as spheres, may be used to shed light on why organizations seem to lose their efficiency as they get larger.

For example, if the company had a total employment T_1 of 100 people, out of which 60 people E_1 would be in the *effective* category, and you wanted to double the size of the company to 200 people T_2. The new number of *effective* personnel would only increase to: $E_2 = 60 (200/100)^{2/3} = 95$ people instead of 2 x 60 = 120 people, as you might have guessed. As a matter of fact, in order to double the production, i.e., to have 120 effective personnel, you have to increase the total employment of the firm to 285 people!

Let's get more specific and define the *The Law of the Sphere*: From the previous area to volume relationship, $A_2/A_1 = (V_2 / V_1)^{2/3}$, where the area of a second sphere is proportional to the area of a first sphere as given by the two-thirds power of the ratio between the volumes of the second to that of the first sphere. This can now be generalized as:

165

The Law of the Sphere

The ratio between a number depending on a second variable to a number depending on a first variable is given by the two-thirds power of the ratio between the second and the first variable, or somewhat simplified: *The ratio of one set of numbers is equal to the two-third's power or the ratio of a second set of numbers*:

$$A_2 / A_1 = (V_2 / V_1)^{2/3}$$

Now if we want to know what A_2 is, we rearrange the equation as follows:

$$A_2 = A_1(V_2 / V_1)^{2/3}.$$

Now let's apply this law to human organizations by substituting, for example, the number of total workers for volume and the number of effective workers for area. We now can determine the ratio between the two if a company grows, i.e., the total number of workers increases from size (1) to size (2). So we may state:

$$\frac{\text{No. of effective workers}(2)}{\text{No. of effective workers}(1)} = \left(\frac{\text{No. of total workers}(2)}{\text{No. of total workers}(1)}\right)^{2/3}$$

Instead of dealing with individual persons, we may substitute a group of workers, such as a department. We, thus, could say there are 12 total departments including 7 effective departments in Plant A and 20 total departments in Plant B. Then all things being equal, what would be the number of effective departments in Plant B?

The solution is:

$(20/12)^{2/3}$ x 7 = 9.84, or rounded, 10 effective departments.

If we want to apply this law to the military (and we may as well), it is easy to substitute the number of effective units, such as companies or divisions for plant departments. Here is an example:

In 1997 there were approximately 495,000[*] men and women who served in the U.S. Army. Let's assume the largest, *effective* fighting organization "Y" is a Division (about 14,000 soldiers). Looking at these numbers you would guess the total number of divisions, "X" that can be fielded are 495,000 divided by 14,000 which rounded off is 35. Unfortunately, this number is not correct. So let's consult the *Law of the Sphere*: Here, $X = 1 \times (495,000/14,000)^{2/3} = 10.8$ Divisions. This compares well with recent press reports that the U.S., at present, has 10 combat-ready divisions. The above relationship sadly indicates that simply doubling the size of the Army would not double the number of combat-ready divisions. It would only increase it to: $X = 1 \times (990,000/14,000)^{2/3} = 17.1$ or 17 divisions (rounded off) instead of 22! If we multiply the 10.8 Divisions by 14,000 personnel each, we get 151,200 fighting personnel out of a total of 495,000, or one out of 3.3. Contrast this to the

---

[*] *The New York Times*, April 29, 1997.

ancient Chinese army[*], which in about 400 B.C. had three fighting men out of every four.

You may think, well, this is the government---private industry is much more efficient. Perhaps not always. Consider, for example, the German Volkswagen Company. Ferdinand Porsche designed the original *Beetle* Volkswagen between 1934 and 1936, had the first prototype on the road in 1936, and the first production run of 30 cars assembled by April 1937. He was able to do this with about 50 technicians and engineers and at a cost (at today's dollars) of about $23 million.[**]

In contrast, in the 1970s, the Volkswagen Company employed about 50,000 engineers and technicians. Despite this, the company was unable to design a suitable replacement for the then obsolete *Beetle*. In desperation, VW then purchased a German competitor, Auto Union and utilizing the "NSU" Construction, sold it under the name of Rabbit. It was curious, but you could still see the Auto Union's *Olympic Rings* trademark on the car engines produced by VW during the first two years. Why should this be? Consider the law of the sphere. By increasing the engineering staff from 50 to 50,000, the Volkswagen Company only increased the number of effective engineers by $(50,000/50)^{2/3} = 100$ times, instead of the

[*] Sun Tzu, *The Art of War*, (Oxford University Press), 1963. p. 72.
[**] Mommsen, Hans, "Das Volkswagenwerk und Seine Arbeiter im dritten Reich," *Econ Verlag*, 1966.

1,000 fold increase it expected. Apparently this was not enough.

Obviously, some companies might be more efficient than others and may be able to maintain a higher ratio of effective to supportive labor than indicated by the mathematical relationship of a pure sphere. However, I maintain that it will be impossible for even the best manager to maintain a *constant* ratio when his company grows. What he may be able to do is maintain a larger exponential growth factor. Table 12-1 shows the mathematical relationship assuming the *worst* or *basic* exponent factor of 2/3 dictated by the *Law of the Sphere* as previously discussed (A), or a factor of ¾ (B), *better*, or if you are really *tops*, then you might manage a 7/8 factor (C).

Table 12-1

Relationship between increases in effective labor to overall employment

A) Standard efficiency organization, n = 2/3 per the *Law of the Sphere*

If total employment is increased by a factor of:	2	5	10	20	50	100
Then effective labor increases by a factor of:	1.6	2.9	4.6	7.4	13.6	21.5

B) Better efficiency organization, n = ¾

If total employment is increased by a factor of:	2	5	10	20	50	100
Then effective labor increases by a factor of:	1.7	3.3	5.6	9.5	18.8	31.6

C) Optimum efficiency organization, n = 7/8

If total employment is increased by a factor of:	2	5	10	20	50	100
Then effective labor increases by a factor of:	1.8	4.1	7.5	13.8	30.7	56.2

I consider an optimum baseline to be 65 effective persons out of a total employment of 100. Using the data from Table 12-1 (A), we can now derive the exact number of effective workers out of a total work force and derive the E/S ratio (the ratio of effective over supportive workers).

Table 12-2

Total employees:	100	200	500	1000	2000	5000
Effective employees:	65	104	189	299	481	884
Supportive employees:	35	96	311	701	1519	4116
E/S ratio:	1.86	1.08	0.61	0.43	0.32	0.21

As you can see, there has to be a dramatic increase in production efficiency for the effective workers in plants with over 500 people in order to make up for the drastic increase in overhead (number of supportive employees). Hence, increase in manufacturing efficiency barely keeps up with increase in administrative expenses. The above table also demonstrates quite vividly why smaller companies are able to compete successfully against industrial giants.

The question for the CEO is what category does his or her company fall under. One source for the answer is obviously the profit and loss statement. A low profit before earnings and taxes usually means a *bad* ratio between effective and supportive personnel. As a rule of thumb, with a single plant or division having about $20 million in sales, if your operating profit before tax is 2% or less, you definitely have a low efficiency exponent. If profits are up to 10%, you probably fall into the better category, and with profits exceeding

171

15%, you certainly are in the optimum efficiency category. There may, of course, be extenuating circumstances that distort your profit picture such as a strike or a recession; therefore, it is best to use five-year averages. Of course, you may throw this book away, if you run a multi-billion dollar a year software business as a monopoly and business efficiency is of no concern, as long as you can dictate the price.

Now back to us folks who have to compete. Another way to judge your firm is to divide the effective number into the total number of employees. Use 100 total and 65 effective as a basis,[*] then consult Table 12-1 and see where you stand.

For example: Your total employment is 980 of which 310 are classified as effective. Now your total employment has increased by 980/100 = 9.8 times, and the number of effective workers by 310/65 = 4.8 times using the bench mark numbers (i.e., 100 and 65) from Table 12-2 (first column). Looking at Table 12-1, we find that in Group (A), the effective increase for a ten times increase in employment would have been 4.6. In Group (B), it is 5.6. So you fall somewhere in between.

The base figures of 100 for total and 65 for effective employees re somewhat arbitrary and would certainly vary by industry. If you run a multi-divisional enterprise, then you could use the smaller, or most

---

[*] I consider 65 effective out of a total employment of 100 an optimal number for a manufacturing plant.

172

efficient, division as a baseline in order to do a similar analysis.

The main point here is that as with living organisms, there is an inherent law that growth and efficiency cannot be scaled up at the same rate.

To keep growing and yet stay in Group (C) instead of Group (A) takes the talent of a superb manager. Simply increasing profit with increasing sales is not enough. Being able to increase profits *at the same rate* is what truly separates a great manager from a mediocre one.

Returning back to business, here is an example of a valve and fitting business listed on the New York Stock Exchange and run by a very capable CEO. His growth record (mainly by acquisitions) is outstanding and showed an annual compounded growth rate of 16.6% over the past 15 years. Yet, his net profit grew only at a compounded rate of 14.5%! Since we may assume that profit is directly related to the ratio of effective to supportive personnel, then we may apply the *Law of the Sphere* just as well to the ratio between profit and sales volume, as long as the relationship between sales and number of effective workers remains constant.[*]

Let's examine the facts as stated in the company's annual report for 1997. In Figure 12-4, I have plotted

---

[*] This, of course, implies that the number of supportive personnel increases exponentially in respect to sales volume.

net profit versus annual sales. As you can see, the number conforms well to the general trend given by the *Law of the Sphere* where 1997 profit = 1982 profit[*] x (Sales 1997/Sales 1982)$^{2/3}$. I can well sympathize with this CEO's level of frustration. The percentage of profit keeps slipping despite his best efforts not realizing he is up against a natural law! And while his aim is to reach a sales volume of $1 billion before the second millennium (up from the present $720 million), he may only reach a net profit of 6.5% of sales as compared to the present 7.2% following the dictates of this law unless, of course, the IRS changes his tax bracket.

This example shows that in the absence of knowledge about the number of the supportive and effective personnel, the sales to profit relationship may be used as an analytical tool using the *Law of the Sphere*.

Unfortunately, it is nearly impossible to find exact and published reports on the ratio between *effective* and *supportive* personnel. We do, however, find published data between profit (either as a total sum, or as a percentage of sales) and the total employment figures of firms.

---

[*] Increased to fit curve averages.

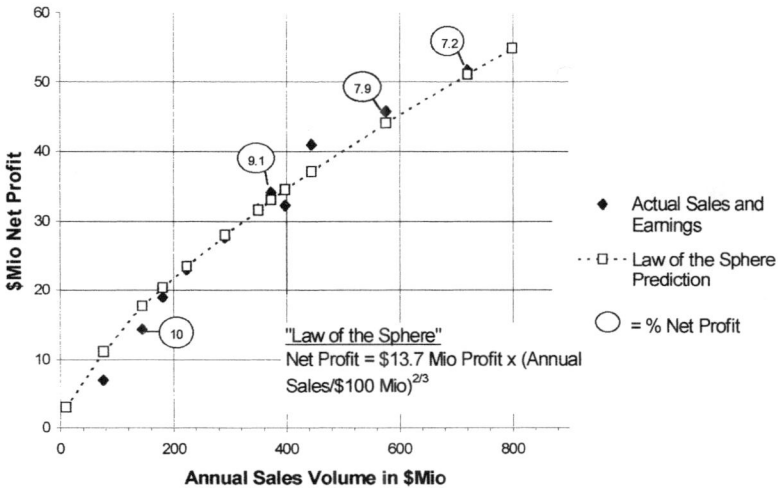

Figure 12-4 Sales volume and profit before tax of a manufacturing company listed on the New York Stock Exchange. Note, profit as percentage of sales declined with company growth, even though overall profit increased. This indicates a decrease in efficiency.

With few exceptions, the profit of a company is always low if the total employment is too high. In other words, companies employ too many people than are required to provide goods or services at competitive prices. Exceptions arise, for example, if the company rents expensive office space, or their business is based on importing hardware or material from a country whose currency value has increased substantially vis-à-vis the U.S. dollar. Nevertheless, these exceptions should not detract us from the overall

175

relationship of the number of employees versus profit. Such a relationship can reflect the otherwise invisible ratio between *effective* and *supportive* personnel.

In my experience, it is very rare that the number of hours used to produce a certain part by an *effective* person varies between a small and a larger company. Such similarity, at least in the manufacturing sector, is already dictated by the use of machine tools, which are all run automatically and at optimum speed.

Hence, our conclusion has to be that the *only* reason why profit decreases in larger organizations is that the number of *supportive* personnel increases out of proportion to the necessary increase in the number of *effective* personnel. This becomes apparent when we analyze the dollar sales per person per year[*] versus the size of the company expressed in the number of total employees. Figure 12-5 shows such a relationship. While there is quite a scattering of the available data from manufacturing companies, the trend is unmistakable. Again, the sales volume per employee decreases drastically (and thereby the companies' profit) with the increase in the size of a given company, or division, as expressed by its number of employees. Again, the *Law of the Sphere* can be used as a tool to at least explain and predict this trend.

---

[*] Defined as the yearly sales volume in U.S. dollars of a company divided by the average number of total employees of the same company.

A WORD OF CAUTION: Exponential curves or equations cannot be extended ad infinitum. Reasonable benchmarks should be set for each individual case.

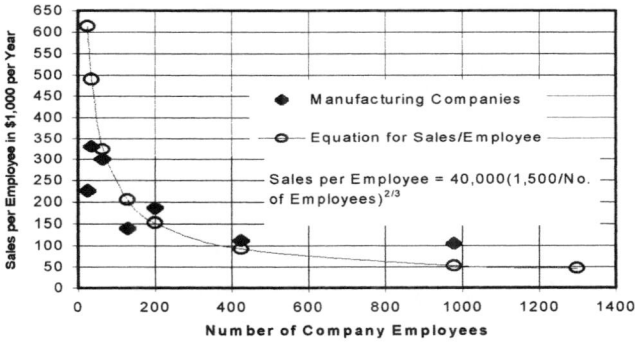

Figure 12-5   Relationship between sales per employee and total number of company employees. Smaller companies have more sales per employee, hence, more profitability.

The projected value of $386,000 per 50 employees (in 1997 dollars) in Figure 12-5 (smooth line) may already be too high since such a limit is set by the physical capacity of an individual worker or his or her machine tool. On the other side of the spectrum, there may not be any company with sales of less than $70,000 per employee. If it existed before, it is probably bankrupt now. Another reason why we have companies still in business with very low sales per employee (see the entry in Figure 12-5 for 1,000 employees) is that such a company may be located in a low wage area of the United Sates with average yearly wages of perhaps $25,000 per employee instead of $50,000 in high cost areas. This then would distort the statistics accordingly. This would mask otherwise equivalent higher wage sales per employee of the otherwise only $50,000.

As in nature, nothing is exactly predictable. On the other hand, nothing in nature follows linear relationships and, as the graphs in this chapter clearly show, neither is the relationship linear between company size (number of employees) and profit. The reader may rightfully argue that the *Law of the Sphere* is not applicable in all cases, and he may be right. But even the most skeptical reader should admit that an exponential relationship does exist. If so, then we only argue about the numerical value (or values) of the exponential factor in our equation.

Remember, all our effort in controlling human economic endeavor is really an attempt to understand and to control chaos.

How to reverse the process

Any good manager having *inherited* a large company may ask him or herself the question: Can the process of exponential administrative growth be reversed? The answer is...probably not. One may consider splitting the company in two or three parts (if this is possible from the given product structure. This is a so-called *de-merger*, a ploy not so much exercised to gain efficiency (which it does not do, see explanation below), but to gamble that the stock market value of each of the individual new divisions combined will exceed the stock value of the old parent company.

Why does a de-merger not improve efficiency? For example, let's assume you split a company with two independently run divisions, each having 8% after tax profit, in half. There is no reason to expect that the profit of each of these divisions will increase dramatically after the split-up. For an explanation let's consult the *Law of the Sphere*. If you divide a large sphere (the parent company) into, say, two equal halves, you still get the same ratio between *effective* and total personnel (ratio between curved surface area and volume). For example, Company *A* has 10,000 employees. According to the $2/3^{rd}$ *Law of the Sphere*, (*see* Table 12-1), there are about 2,200 effective employees (using 100 as base level) and 7,800 supportive employees, or a ratio of about 3.5 supportive to 1 effective. If you split this company *A* into two equal parts *B* and *C*, then each of *B* and *C* has 1,100 effective and 3,900 supportive personnel...still a ratio of 3.5 to 1!

In contrast, if *B* and *C* had grown by itself from humble beginnings to a total of 5,000 employees each, they would have had 1,357 *effective* and 3,643 *supportive* personnel, or a ratio of only 2.68 to 1. This could have improved the productivity and, therefore, the profit before tax by [(1357 / 1100) x 100] - 100 = 23%. Alas, you can never start all over. So what are our choices?

179

Well, one way to keep growing efficiently while at the same time improving your bottom line is to grow sideways. What I mean by this is to buy one or more smaller competitors, preferably in the $50 million or below sales range (that is before they too become *water logged.*) The trick here is to maintain their independence. The temptation is usually too irresistible for the staff people of the larger parent company (the buyer) to impose their own *good will* onto the unfettered hierarchy of the smaller purchased company. Such impositions start from the most innocent requests for a *uniform financial reporting system* (with the resultant need for a brand new computer system) to environmental regulations, patent systems, *combined* purchasing efforts, prescribed engineering and drafting practices, to more hurtful pressures on inventory levels. All this is usually done behind the back of the CEO of the parent company, who is, most of the time, quite a common sense type of a person.

The requests are quite innocuous starting with a simple e-mail message from corporate headquarters. How long can the new General Manager (usually an up and coming executive from the parent company) refuse such a request? Usually not for very long, if he still wants to be considered a *team player*! This means interference from his own staff has to be strongly opposed by the parent company's CEO. This should be rule number one.

Rule number two is to limit the growth of the acquired company to a manageable level and then start a new

180

practical company, typically by splitting up parts of the product lines of the original company. What you should do is clone, and upon growth, keep on cloning the well-run new division.

The following is an example of how a small, acquired company with, say, 100 people, of whom 60 are in the effective and 40 are in the supportive categories can grow. Assume further that the company has $25 million in yearly sales. Expenses are 32% labor, 20% material, and 20% others. This leaves a profit before taxes of 28% or $7 million. Now let's look at two different approaches to growth. Assume the acquiring corporation is well-run and falls in the *excellent* category where the number of effective personnel grows by a factor of 0.875 (modified spherical law), or $X = Y(B/A)^{7/8}$ where X is the number of effective employees and B is the total number of employees. Assume further that the labor efficiency and the cost per employee ($80,000 per person) stay the same. The reference number A is 100 from above and the number of effective employees Y is 60.

Table 12-3 shows the number of effective employees using the above equations plus the resultant profit for companies that keep on growing as a single entity or subsidiary.

One can clearly see what happens here. Despite a great and well-run central management team (7/8 factor), the percent of profit degenerates steadily and there will be a loss once employment exceeds 13,500. Incidentally, using an exponential factor of 2/3 (the true sphere), the company would already be in the red at only 3,000 employees!

Table 12-3

Company Size (# of persons)[1]	Yearly Sales ($mio)[2]	No. of Effec. Personnel "X"	No. of Supp. Personnel	Total Wages[3] ($ mio)	Material & Other (40%)	Profit	
						$ mio	%
100	25	60	40	8	10.0	7	28
200	46	110	90	16	18.4	11.6	25
400	84	202	198	32	34	18	21
800	154	370	430	64	62	28	18
1600	282	679	921	128	113	41	15
3200	519	1245	1955	256	208	55	10
6400	951	2283	4117	512	380	59	6
12800	1745	4188	8612	1024	698	23	1.3

[1] Total employment
[2] $417,000 per effective employee
[3] $80,000 per employee

To contrast this, let's assume we will split up each subdivision once the employment figures exceed 200 (the *cloning* approach).

As you can see from Figure 12-6, when the overall employment reaches 800, you have five independent (or more) operating subdivisions with total sales of $188 million and a pre-tax operating profit of $49 million (26%). Contrast this with the single company with the same 800 people from Table 12-2 having sales of $154 million and a profit before tax of only $28 million (18%)!

This may be an idealized case, not all cloned divisions grow at the same rate for example. Nevertheless, it serves as a guide on how to approach the problem of finding a way to stay efficient while growing. The ultimate success of this approach depends on grooming good general managers who are adept at understanding the philosophy of staying *lean* and who are willing to maintain the proven management organization and style of the originally cloned successful division.

Total $ Sales	Profit $	% Profit	Total Eff. Employees	Total Employees
25	7	28	60	100
46	11.6	25	110	200
96	25.6	27	230	400
138	34.8	25	330	600
188	49	26	450	800

Original Plant

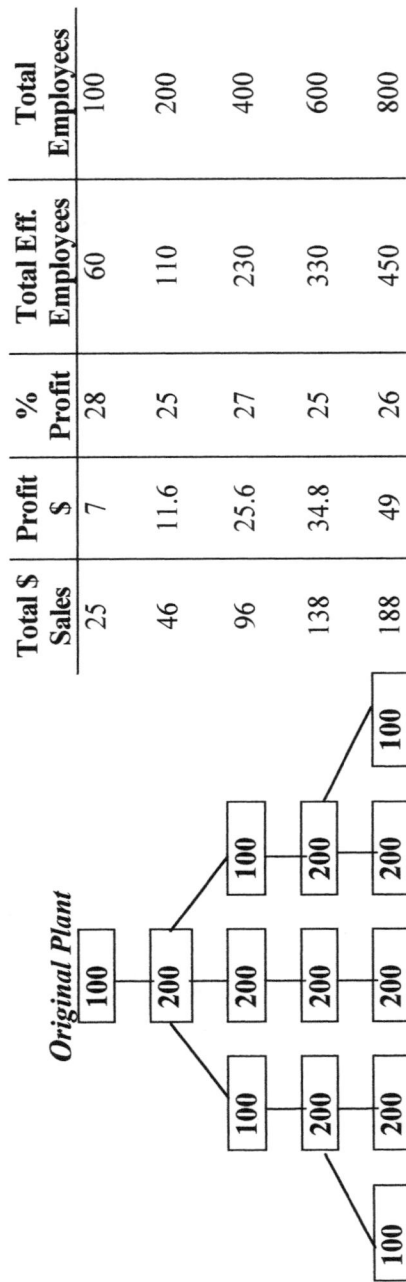

All sales and profit numbers are in $ millions. Numbers in brackets are total employees per plant.

Figure 12-6 How cloning a company can maintain high profitability while increasing sales volume. In this example, an initial plant with 100 employees evolves into five separate plants with a total of 800 employees.

Chapter 13

Mergers And Acquisitions

A merger of equals is never what it seems.

In any merger, there are never any equals despite pre-merger protestation. Invariably, after about 6 months, there is a power struggle between the two company CEOs with the weaker of the two departing the new and larger company solaced by being paid off with umpteen million dollars of *golden parachute* funds. As in politics, there are no two equal rulers.

There are usually three reasons for companies to merge or to acquire typically smaller companies: First is the growth in sales volume. This impresses the shareholders and usually enhances their stock value on Wall Street. Second, mergers improve the financial clout of a company when it comes to borrowing or floating new stock or bonds. You have to be careful with acquisitions since funds may have to be borrowed in order to finance the acquisition.

185

The interest on those loans depresses your income, and the principle increases your company's liability, especially if the acquisition price was at a premium. Third, and this is seldom admitted, an acquisition or merger is often used to increase the market share of your company in a given line of products. This can get dicey if such a market share gets too big leading to becoming a monopoly. Typically, the government's Anti-trust Department will try to prevent this.

When I was vice president of a larger firm, part of my job was to look out for suitable acquisition candidates. Invariably, I always discovered two problems especially with smaller firms. The first is that when a company is very profitable, it is well run, usually by an entrepreneur-type individual running a lean organization. Based on his profit level (may be 30% before tax), he will demand a very high multiple to his company's book value or sales volume per year. For example, if profit B.I.T. is 30% of sales and the seller demands a price equivalent of 20 times earnings, this would be $20 \times 30\%/100\% = 6$ times sales. This reduces the return on acquisition capital to 5% B.I.T. One solution to this dilemma is to increase sales using the marketing power of your own (the buyer's) organization.

However, there is a second problem, which is finding a suitable replacement for the (usually soon-departing) president of the acquired company. According to Mark Herndorn of Watson Wyatt Worldwide in Dallas, Texas, 47% of acquired executives leave in the first year and 75% leave within the first 3 years. That means you have the daunting task of finding a qualified person in your own organization. Finding a less qualified individual will surely increase bureaucracy and inefficiency by simply following the habits and customs of your own (typically much larger and less profitable company). For more details, see the chapter on the Law of the Sphere.

Another problem I encountered, or better yet, the second type of seller I encountered was a not so well-run enterprise, which was either close to bankruptcy or had marginal profit rates of 5% B.I.T. or less. The invariable reason was bad management. Again, the problem is how to find a suitable manager to run this company once you buy it. The selling price is usually book value or one times annual sales, so this is not such a big problem, but reducing the number of employees of such an inefficiently run company (the key to better profitability) certainly is.

Due Diligence for companies having marginal profitability is especially important. Some of the marginal profit may only exist in non-sellable inventory, for example. So paradoxically as it sounds, the cheap acquisition can turn out to be the major headache (better you pay a premium for the good one).

In the previous chapter, you were told that increasing the company's size would eventually reduce profit. This is true if a company grows at a monolithic entity, but not necessarily if it grows simply by adding a string of other semi-independent companies to your corporate corral. This is very similar to the solution of using cloning discussed in the Law of the Sphere chapter.

Consider the corporate umbrella as the thread through a string of pearls as shown in Figure 11-2. As in nature, each pearl has its own special size and luster. Consider each pearl as an individual, semi-independent division, which has its own size and profit level. It even helps to maintain their previous company names and logos! As long as each division does not grow very fast or their product lines do not become obsolete, their profit will remain fairly constant, barring a recession or other major disruptions.

The profit of the corporate parent, the owner of the string of pearls, simply reports the average profit of all those individual pearls (divisions). The example in Figure 11-2 shows a total of 17 pearls or divisions having a total, yearly sales volume of $1581 million. Assume further that the *average* profit before tax is 16.5%. The president decides to buy another company having a sales volume of $150 million per year at a rate of profit of 15.9%.

This will increase parent company's next year's sales to 1581 + 150 = $1731 million and the overall rate of profit to (0.165% x 1581)+ (0.159 x 150) / 173 = 0.164, i.e. 16.4%.

Making another acquisition or merger (if skillfully done) will just add another pearl (division) to the string. If the last pearl is especially bright (division with above average earnings), then this will add to the overall luster of the pearls, i.e., the corporate profit average will increase. This is good corporate strategy because by enlarging your corporation through mergers and acquisitions, you will show your shareholders a continuous increase in sales volume and profit. That the percentage profit stays fairly level, as explained previously, need not be advertised. What Wall Street is looking for is the price/earning ratio. This is independent of percentage of profit on sales and as long as you add one additional pearl to your string, your profit *sum* will go up and so will your share price if the P/E ratio remains constant unless you float more stock and dilute your earnings.

For example, your sales last year were $5 billion and profit $500 million (10% profit). Based on a price/earnings (P/E) ratio of 20, your stock may be worth 20 x $500 million = $10 billion (this is called market capitalization). This year you buy a new company with $500 million sales and a profit of $60 million financed by loans. Now your total sales grew by 10% to $5.5 billion and your profit to $560 million. This will now demand a new stock price of 20 x $560 million or $11.2 billion. Note that your stock value grew from $10 to $11.2 billion, a 12% increase even though your *percentage* of profit only changed from 10% to 10.18%, or hardly at all. Overall, it is a good strategy that is employed by a number of successful companies such as General

Electric and Emerson Electric Co. Not surprisingly, it takes people with vision to run those companies (not to mention a phenomenal memory to keep everything in focus!).

Figure 11-3 in Chapter 11 shows an impressive and consistent growth record in both sales and in total profit of one typical company that has a successful merger and acquisition strategy. However, a larger corporate umbrella does not guarantee a growth in *percent* of profit. Figure 11-3 shows the rather impressive growth in *total after tax profit*, which increased in the 15 years between 1983 and 1998 from $330 to $1229 million; a feat that makes the heart of each Wall Street analyst beat faster. Yet if you analyze the percent of *profit before income tax* (I use this because the effective tax rate decreased from 43.9% in 1983 to 36.1 % in 1998.), you will see in Figure 11-4 that this percentage decreased from 15.4% in 1983 to 14.3% in 1998. This is certainly not a ringing endorsement of the often-held theory that there is greater cost efficiency with an increase in size. Yet, the management of this company should be congratulated for this achievement despite the almost four-fold growth in size during the past 15 years realizing that each acquired subsidiary adds more complexity to the already barely manageable complex. The nagging question is: Would the overall profit level of each of the acquired companies be higher if they would have been left alone? We will never know the answer!

As you can see, aside from economically caused fluctuations, the percent profit level stays essentially flat as explained above.

Now to the not so successful mergers and acquisitions.

Bad Mergers

According to Cornelius Grove & Associates LLC, as reported in the March 2000 issue of *Business NH Magazine* mergers and acquisitions have unfavorable impact on profitability and are strongly associated with lower productivity, labor unrest, high absenteeism and poor accident rates. According to Mercer Management Consultants, Inc., and as stated in the same issue, about 50% of all mergers fail to meet expectations.

So let us start out with leveraged buyouts. You may not want to read on, if you are one of the few individuals who can pat their wallets with satisfaction because you owned the shares of the company, which was taken over at a grossly overpaid price tag. The story is less cheerful for those who held the shares of the company that did the buying.

The mood of the acquired company's employees is also not too cheerful. Notice, whenever such a merger is announced, there is always talk of eliminating several thousand jobs to save umpteen million dollars. Luckily for those employees, it is mostly talk to impress Wall Street. Even if employees of the newly joined company are laid off to *save* money, substantial sums are spent on consultants in order to figure out how to make all this work.

As stated by David McCourt, the chairman of RCN in the *New York Times* on August 27, 1998, "AT&T announces a takeover of TCT; Bell Atlantic, which is still adjusting to its acquisition of Nynex, merges with GTE; SBC Communication buys Pacific Telesis and then Ameritech.

The list goes on and on, but these deals share one trait (beyond paying the greens fees of lawyers and investment bankers)---they probably won't work." All I can add to this is *Amen!*

Banks are a good example of bad mergers. When two regional banks merge they typically combine their headquarter staff but close, you guessed it, their branch offices replacing them with ATM machines. The branch offices are the outer layer of the sphere (total company) and this is where the daily business occurs and where the profit comes from. This is comparable to the sales department of a manufacturing company. Yet, looking at the *Law of the Sphere*, this closure of bank offices is pre-programmed. Take two banks A and B of equal size, say 500 employees (as shown in Figure 13-1) of which 250 in each bank work in branch offices (surface area of each sphere). After a merger of the two banks, the new *volume* of the sphere (total employment of the company) is 2 x 500 = 1,000.

192

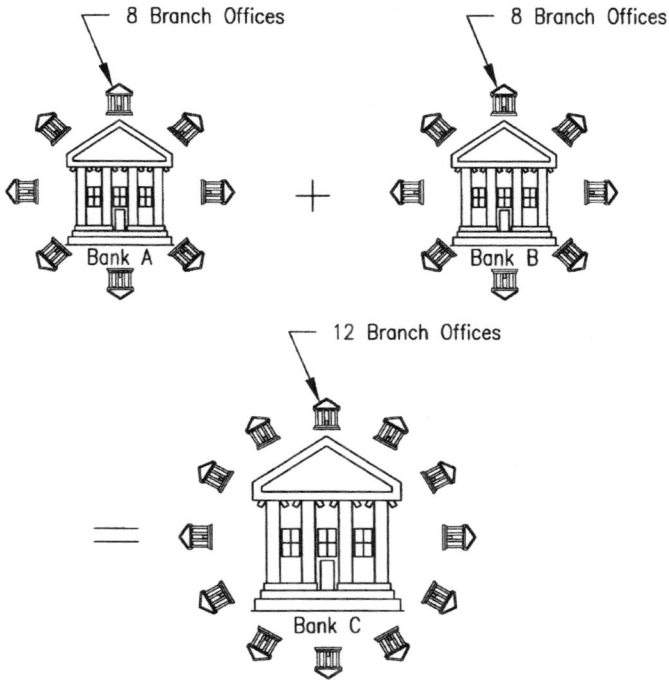

Figure 13-1 Example of the merger of two equally sized banks. Per the Law of the Sphere, new number of branches declines to 12.7 when calculated. Number after merger = 8 x $2^{2/3}$ = 12.7. This agrees with the graphic demonstration shown above.

The new surface area per our law should now be $(1,000/500)^{2/3}$ x (250) = 397. Since the old number of branch office employees was 2 x 250 = 500 employees, you have to lay off 500 - 397= 103 employees or 10.3% of the total work force. This is what typically happens, as you well know from reading the local papers. Figure 13-1 shows the home office/branch office relationship in a simplified graphical form for easy understanding.

You start with two equally sized branches A and B each having eight branch offices. You now merge these two banks and in the process create a new bank C. This doubles the volume (total employment) of bank C over that of A or B. Now a sphere has to increase its diameter about 1.26 times (since volume is a function of the cube of the diameter, hence 1.26 x 1.26 x 1.26 = 2). We, therefore, draw a circle around bank C that is 26% larger than that for bank A or B.

Notice that we have space for only about 12 equally sized branch offices around the circumference of bank C reducing the overall number before the merger from 16 (2 x 8) to 12. To be exact, and using the *Law of the Sphere*, the new number of branch offices = old number per bank x (number of banks)$^{2/3}$ or NEW = 8 x $(2)^{2/3}$ = 12.7 post merger branches. This is a reduction of 20.6%! Most of them are people in the "effective" (i.e., profit producing) category. Since 50% of all employees worked in branch offices, the number of laid off employees is 50% of 20.6% = 10.3% as explained previously.

A case in point is a news item that appeared in the April 3, 1999 issue of *The Economist*, which stated: "*Bank One* is to cut about 4,000 jobs, 4% of their work force, and take a $526 million charge in the aftermath of its $20.7 billion merger with *First Chicago*." This after they already took a $984 million charge in the fourth quarter of 1998 making the total loss $1.51 billion or 7.3% of the original purchase price with probably more to come!

Coming back to our example, you may wonder what happens to the profit (we now have 103 less profit producing or *effective* employees). Banks have to raise their fees to cover this deficiency in income. Looking at our bank statements, we are all aware of this trend! According to the *Palm Beach Post* of April 12, 1999, a Federal Reserve study showed that bigger banks, including those created by mergers, tend to charge higher fees than smaller ones. At commercial banks, in 1998 net interest income totaled $174.5 billion, but fee income grew to $104.5 billion (a growth of 150% during the past 10 years when bank mergers accelerated). More specific examples are stated in the February 5th issue of TIME magazine:

BANK FEES:	Small Banks	Large Banks
Low-balance, non-interest check fees:	$ 5.62	$ 8.20
Stop payment order:	$ 13.92	$ 21.50
ATM withdrawals at other banks:	$ 1.09	$ 1.32

Another example of a bad merger that could not be cured by fee increases was R.J.R. Nabisco, the leveraged buyout that made history in 1985. The company has since split up after being saddled with high debt financed by junk bonds. Other companies were not that lucky. According to KDP Investment Advisors, Montpelier, Vermont[*], of 25 cases between

---

[*] *New York Times*, March 14, 1999. p. 8.

1985 and 1989 where companies were saddled with more than $1 billion in debt, almost half defaulted on their loans. Even more filed for bankruptcy or had to sell off assets.

There are ample signs that mega-mergers don't work. DuPont wants to split off its remaining 70% share of Conoco, Inc. and Hewlett-Packard Company did sell off a portion of their $7.6 billion a year business that produces test and measurement equipment, just to name a few.

The managerial complexity of big mergers can be mind blowing. When Citibank merged with Travelers, they learned they had 150,000 different types of accounts (accounting ledgers) requiring 28 different computer systems!

According to the June 5, 1999 issue of *The Economist*, due to mergers in the European insurance industry, the market share of the top five insurers in Britain has risen from 22% in 1990 to 36% in 1998, yet the overhead expenses as a percent of premium have gone up from 29% to 33%. This is not a ringing endorsement of *bigger is better*.

As with all things in life, what goes up must come done. Merger mania will create firms so large that (absence of monopolistic market dominance), their complexity and inefficiency will reach a no longer sustainable level and, as a last resort, they will de-merge again.

Remember large corporations can only survive by being a conglomerate of numerous quasi-autonomous divisions or subdivisions, or by splitting themselves up into separate divisions such as the Cadillac division of General Motors. Bigness certainly has its price!

With the price of oil again up, we might as well focus on the oil production industry. Here we have seen a consolidation, i.e. mergers between most major multinational corporations such as Exxon and Mobil. The purported reason is to reduce expenses of staff and pool resources for oil exploration, all supposed to benefit the shareholders.

Alas, the opposite may happen. According to Bill Fairhurst[*] such mergers do not increase the value of the new company greater than the sum of the individual parts, nor have resources of oil or gas been added to satisfy our ever-increasing demands. Additionally, the share price of many multinational oil companies have under-performed the Dow Jones Industrial Average by 50% and have not kept up with inflation during the 11-year period ending December 31, 2000.

What is worse is that the bulk of the integrated and multi-national oil companies on average only replace 44% of their yearly production of oil or gas while

---

[*] Fairhurst, Bill, "Why US Energy Policy and Wall Street Should Focus on US Independents," *Oil & Gas Journal*, July 30, 2001.

smaller independent companies average a 131% replacement rate!

According to Bill Fairhurst, the (much smaller) independents add more reserves within the United States than all the large multinational corporations combined. This is despite the fact that the larger corporations spent much more money on exploration cost. The data in Figure 13-2 and taken from Fairhurst's article shows this graphically.

Here four, large multi-nationals and five, large integrated oil companies spent on average $1.70 per thousand cubic feet of gas equivalent (Mcfe) and in the process average less than 50% replacement of what they produce (sell). In contrast, the smaller and mid-size independents average 100% replacement with a cost of only $1.30 per Mcfe.

Even though these data points are quite naturally scattered, the alert reader may spot a familiar trend. Again, why not use the "Law of the Sphere" as a model and try to predict this trend. Indeed, this seems to work quite well, as you can see from the prediction curve superimposed in Figure 13-2.

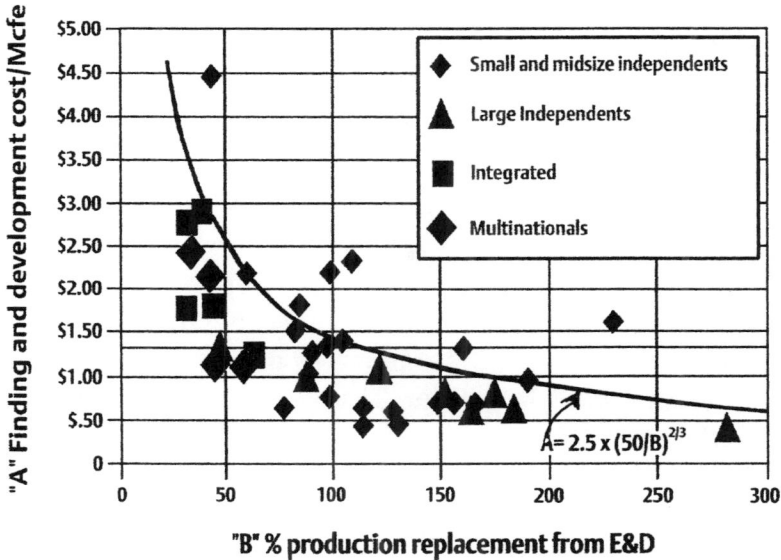

Figure 13-2 Finding/developmental cost for 37 companies when compared to results in % production replacement.

The lessons learned in this case?

1. Try not to merge unless you are in dire straits such as having depleted all your resources of oil and gas.

2. As a large corporation try to subcontract all your exploration activity out to smaller independent operators. Buying out smaller independents (a typical solution for multinationals in order to increase their reserves of oil and gas) is at best a short-term solution since soon the newly

199

acquired companies will become just as inefficient as their new parent company.

So far I have commented on the dismal economic aspects of mergers. But there are more sinister by-products that primarily affect the shareholders of the companies involved in mergers. Typically, at least one of the merger partners obtains additional loans to pay for the significant legal and underwriting expenses that have to be paid in order to consummate the merger, but also for the sometimes multi-million dollar bonuses paid to the top management of the surviving merger partner. This is in addition to the sometimes equally high "golden parachute" severance payment to the management of the acquired merger partner. Of course, all this has been pre-arranged by the parties in this deal. Quite often the underwriter (broker) is also the bank providing the loan, so they don't complain.

What we have here is management going into a merger arrangement having no demonstrable economic purpose, saddling the company with unnecessary debt (the service of the debit will depress future earnings and the balance sheet), and getting rich in the bargain!

The sufferers in this deal are the shareholders. What can you do? Vote "no" when you are asked to approve the merger. The next time you get one of those proxy voting forms, exercise your rights and vote "no" for all directors at the next annual election of all companies that are involved in the merger.

Other than that, you can join a class action lawsuit to sue the management. The problem with this is that even if monies are recovered, the lion share goes to the attorneys and you will see only a pittance. In addition, this money does not come from the offending officers of the company but from the corporate coffers, thereby, leading to greater dilution of your share values. Sometimes it seems you cannot win!

Chapter 14

How The Government Can Help You

Government legislated assistance is the only help a Businessperson is forced to accept.

The above title sounds like an oxymoron and in some cases it is since the endless stream of mostly federal government regulations, but eagerly copied on the state and even local government[*] levels, can stifle private enterprise, or at least make it very expensive to conduct business.

All government regulations or census requests start (as do some wars nowadays) from very noble

---

[*] There are now about 80,000 separate governmental entities in the United States according to Alex N. Pattakos as stated in "Rediscovering the Soul of Business," *New Leader Press*, Sterling Stone, Inc., San Francisco, CA, 1995.

intentions. The basic and most common reason for the issuance of a new regulation is to *aid* business. Another reason is to help or protect the workers. Additional regulations are intended, for example, to help collect taxes or duties.

Some of those regulations, usually the outgrowth of some legislation passed by congress or state houses, have sound reasoning and actually contribute to the well-being of workers or the economy. Others are not, and can be a gross distortion of the original legislative intent. In any case, there is typically no accounting of what the law or regulation would do in terms of the cost impact on private businesses or the national economy. For example, if one would add up the number of parking spaces for the handicapped and compare it to the actual number of handicapped people in our nation that are able to drive or be driven, the number would startle you. If it would not be politically incorrect, such a study could be the worthy subject of a $50 million federal grant. I am sure you have cruised through a full parking lot at a local shopping mall and spotted the dozens of empty *reserved for handicapped* spaces.

Speaking of federal help, there are clever businesspersons able to take advantage of the seemingly unending federal ways to financially aid *deserving* businesses, beginning with low-cost loans from the Small Business Administration to outright grants (sometimes the result of special effort by the local Senator or Congressman). The problem is that these funds are available only for business owners (or prospective business owners) with access to well-connected law offices that specialize, for a generous fee (which may take the larger portion of the resultant grant) in filling out the required hundreds of pages of supporting documentation for such a grant.

What sometimes makes government laws and regulations so fiendish is that the mere publication of a new regulation in the Federal Register makes you instantly subject to punishment for non-compliance. The simple fact that no human being is able to read the thousands of pages of the Federal Register, which is printed daily, let alone understand their meaning and remember them, is no legal excuse when you are in front of the judge should you get caught for non-compliance.

True to the *Law of the Sphere*, larger countries (like larger companies) have bigger governments, which absorb a larger share of the country's gross national product than a smaller country. A smaller country's bureaucracy intervenes less because it simply does not have a large enough staff to draft regulations.[*]

From a business perspective, we can subdivide laws and regulations into those that are benign (such as fixing the dates of national holidays) and others that can seriously affect our business in the following, detrimental ways:

---

[*] "Little Countries," *The Economist*, January 3, 1998, pp. 67.

1. Absorb extra, otherwise productive, man-hours for awareness or compliance purposes.
2. Require additional operating capital to alter machinery, providing extra access, etc.
3. Mandate extra manufacturing space and building alterations.
4. Force you to redesign or, worse, obsolete your products.
5. Require a usually more costly, revised method of manufacturing.

The main, albeit unintended, negative side effect of governmental regulations is the potential for the demise of small entrepreneurial companies, which unlike larger, well-capitalized competitors don't have the financial or manpower resources to comply with the regulations. This counters the aim of this book. Unable to comply on a small scale, it may force small and efficient companies to sell out or to join others to become larger and less productive in the bargain. Government regulations thus have a double negative effect.

To explain, it is easy for a 2000-employee company to employ an OSHA specialist and somebody who resolves all environmental problems, but quite another matter for a smaller company employing only 20 people. The large company only adds 0.1% to the payroll (2 people out of 2000) while the small company adds 10%! Yet, for all practical purposes, both have to comply with the same regulations.

The effect of this un-proportionally high burden imposed on small entrepreneurs is restricting their growth on which much of our country's wealth depends. Not only do small companies provide new ideas for products and services but small and mid-size companies hire more new employees than do large, established enterprises.

Now a word about census requirements. You may be familiar with the sometimes ten pages of forms that appear in the mail from either the federal or state government with some city forms thrown in. All these forms demonstrate a noble purpose such as spotting economic trends in your business or documenting the employment figures in your community, for example. I suspect another, unstated motive. If it takes five workers in a given agency to evaluate one page of a questionnaire, then it will take at least 25 workers to evaluate five pages. This not only creates job security at this particular agency, but also is a reason for a legitimate request to increase the agency's budget (adding one page requires five more people!). Of course, any questionnaire is not complete without the extra form explaining the *paper saving act.*

A friend of mine handled this matter in his own, down to earth way. He first looked at the fine print at the bottom of the form. If it did not say *failure to comply with this request is punishable by a fine of up to $10,000 for the first offense, etc.*, then he simply deep-sixed the forms in his wastebasket.

Unfortunately, more and more government agencies heard about my friend who fiendishly tried to deprive agency workers to earn their livelihood. Consequently, they persuaded a compliant congress to add the aforementioned penalty clause to most forms. Well, sometimes you can't win.

As an owner or manager of a small business, you should handle governmental regulations as follows:

1. Read a lot to keep yourself informed.
2. Send your entire payroll through an outside firm that specializes in handling your paychecks and all related federal, state, and city forms for a nominal fee.
3. Ask your insurance carrier to fill you in on the latest OSHA requirements.
4. Hire a good consultant or attorney if you are faced with a problem.
5. Read publications published by your trade association.
6. File your old census forms or state questionnaires in a safe place. You will save a lot of time by copying most of the old information the next time around.
7. Don't buy real estate for your new plant without a thorough investigation of the environment (soil, water). When in doubt, lease the land and buildings.
8. Scared of wrongful discharge or sexual harassment suits? Hire as many temporary workers as possible. At least this will give you a first line of defense. (I have known of a

207

company that had the same "temporary" employee for over 30 years!)

Chapter 15

What Do They Mean When They Say…An Irreverent Glossary

"A rose by any other name is just as sweet."
---William Shakespeare

Not too long ago, the government started to define heretofore clearly understood words into new verbiage in order to obscure their true meaning. For example, changing the name of the former, more to the point, War Department, to Defense Department. Unfortunately, corporate America has followed suit.

While most of you may be familiar with at least some of the newly minted expressions, I thought it might be helpful to have some translations handy. They should help you understand what is truly being said in any meeting you attend, especially when you are confronted with unknown acronyms.

A

Action Item
Work assignment for
committee member. Also
serves to help write
agenda for next meeting.

Adaptable Employee
He who changed jobs a
lot.

**Adept at Office
Organizations** To be
familiar with
MICROSOFT OFFICE

B

B2C
A business that sells to
consumers.

Bankruptcy
When there is no more
money left and you are at
the mercy of your
creditors.

Benchmarking
A look at what your
competitors are doing.

Best-cost producer
Being able to purchase
material from the best-
qualified supplier, not
necessarily from the
cheapest supplier.

Board of Directors
A committee that
supervises the company
president whose
members are elected by
the shareholders, but
usually are selected by
the president.

Budget
A yearly sales target
selected by management,
seldom kept if it were not
for price increases and
inflation.

Business ethics
See Criminal Law

C

Capital Asset
Something you buy that
can be depreciated.
Affects only. your cash
flow, not your profit

**Casual Work
Atmosphere**
Pay is too low to dress up
well.

**Chief Information
Officer
  (CIO)**
Top manager for
computer systems. This
person is supported by a
number of consultants for
technical know-how.

210

Co-branding
Advertising campaign
that uses the brand name
of a second firm (usually
a more recognizable
name).

**Committee
Organization**
Structure, in which
groups of individuals
hold joint authority and
responsibility (no single
person can be blamed).

**Computer Aided Design
(CAD)**
Using a mouse instead of
a pencil to create a
drawing.

Competing
A war between
companies conducted
with other means.

Cost of Quality
A misnomer. Should be:
Cost of *no* quality.

Communication Skills
Able to read and send E-
Mail.

Competitive Salary
Remaining competitive
by paying lower wages
than the competition.

Creative Selling
The art of being a
successful salesman.

Cross-functional Team'
Different departments
trying to work together
on a common project. A
good way to create
delays.

Consumer Satisfaction
Being able to reduce the
number of complaints
about your product and
service.

D

Delegation
Unpleasant work
assigned to others.

Deadline
Something to force the
completion of a never-
ending project.

Differentiation
Why my product is better
than yours.

Disintermediation
Crossing out the
mediation clause in your
contract. Means you have
a potential lawsuit that
makes the attorneys
happier.

Downsizing
Laying off employees,
usually those with higher
salaries and more
experience.

Duties will vary
You may have several
bosses

E
Empowering
Letting you decide when
to go to lunch.
Enhance Bottom Line
Reduce cost.
Entrepreneurship
Ability that is lacking in
most managers.
Enterprise System also
Enterprise Computing
Computer version of how
a company is *thought* to
be organized.
Environmental
Technician
Janitor
E-Mail
Method of
communicating via a
computer keyboard
instead of speaking
directly to the person in
the next office.
Executive Assistant
Secretary

F
Fast-Paced Company
One who has no time to
train its employees.

H
Hardware
The portion of a
computer system you can
actually touch.
Human Resources
Department
Personnel Department
Human Resources
Employees

I
IT
Information Technology
Income Statement
Your income and
expenses.
Informal
Communication
   Channels
Gossip
Integrated Marketing
   Communication
(IMC)
Combining all
advertising
Internal Customer
An employee from a
different department.
InternetA computerized
form of simultaneous
communication between
single or multiple
number of persons (or
computers) done by
interconnecting different

computers in a network usually via telephone wires (see e-Mail)

Inventory Control
The art of balancing the purchasing of parts with the shipment of finished goods.

IT Manager
See Manager of Information Technology

ISO 9000
Clever method to enrich consultants.

J

Just-in-Time (JIT)
Near perfect execution of inventory control where actual in-house inventory approaches zero.

L

Leadership
An assumed management ability.

Legacy System
An older computer program that a newer program has to be able to read. Example: Windows 98 has to be able to read a file written on Windows 95.

Local Area Network

(LAN)
A system that connects a number of computers in a given area.

Loss Prevention Specialist
Security guard

M

Marketing Research
An effort to collect data from customers and competitors to help launch your product. To be effective, the person promoting the product should not do it.

Manager of Information Technology. The person you beg for help when your computer breaks down or crashes.

Macroeconomics
The study of the company's finances in view of the national economy.

M-commerce
Mobile electronic commerce. You are buying books via cell-phone, or wireless computers.

Microeconomics

213

The study of whether or not to give you a raise.

Mission Statements
Modern form of company logos. Can be found on the back of business cards.

Morale
Mental attitude of employees, which can be influenced by communication, raises, or bonuses.

N

Negative Deficit
Profit

Negative Economic Growth
Recession

Not-for-profit Organization
Tax exempt enterprises with unusually high advertising budgets and management salaries.

O

Order Processing
Order entry.

Order Fulfillment
The entire process from order entry to the shipment of goods.

Organization Chart

A listing of company managers and their relationship to each other.

Outsourcing
Purchasing goods from somebody else.

Ownership
Taking ownership means you have been assigned a task.

P

Parent Company
An organization that owns a subsidiary.

Performance Appraisal
A method of filling out forms to either deny or grant raises to an employee.

Portfolio Manager
Stockbroker

Positive Cash Flow
Making money without paying taxes.

Price Adjustment
Price increase

Procurement
Purchasing

Problem-Solving Skills
A pre-requisite in a disorganized company.

Product Differentiation

Convincing your customers that your products are better than those of your competitors even though the price might be higher (see creative selling).

Product Launch
Introduction of a new product to the market. Usually done before the product is ready.

Product Liability
A means to extract money from firms or insurance companies, usually based on assumed defects of products.

Production Planning
Telling the machine shop how many parts to produce, or the Purchasing Dept. how much inventory to buy

Pride in Work
Not to be mistaken for "blaming others for my errors".

Productivity
A means to determine profitability

Pure Play

A business that sells only via Internet and does not own a store or sells from a catalog.

R
Re-engineering
Usually means downsizing the company if profit is low.

Reverse Engineering
A fancy way to copy your competitor's products.

Research and Development
Efforts, usually by a team of engineers, to design a new product from specifications developed by a marketing team. Success usually is inverse proportional to the number of team members.

Resume
What people write when company morale is low.

S
Sales Associate
Salesperson

Self-management Team

A group of employees on there own if their manager is absent.

Seller's Market
Where the price of goods can be set without worrying about competitors.

Service Technician
Repairman

Social Responsibility
Management's actions to combat (usually) government perceived misbehavior.

Software
Invisible instructions to tell the computer what to do. Usually written by persons unfamiliar with your business and obsolete at time of purchase.

Solution
A software that is supposed to solve all your problems.

Statistical Quality Control
A fancy name to express the average dimensional error in a machined part's dimension.

Strategic Alliance
Usually long-term purchasing agreement between a seller and a buyer based on a guaranteed price discount.

Strategic Planning
Usually a five-year sales and financial performance forecast.

Ship on Time
Shipping goods on day of promise.

SWOT Analysis
Assessment of company's strengths and weaknesses usually through the eyes of a consultant.

T

Task Specific Role
Execution of action *item* by a committee member.

Team
Group of people on a project and devoid of any personal responsibility for the task.

Team Cohesiveness
Usually enhanced by joint golf games.

Team Leadership
Having the responsibilities of a manager, without the pay.

Telemarketing
People telephoning you during dinner.

Territory Managers
Outside salesmen
**Total Quality
Management (TQM)**
Public expression of
management's
commitment to quality of
its product. Usually an
action of last resort.

V
Variable Cost
Cost of labor and
material usually
overshadowed by fixed
cost (administrative
expenses)
Viral Marketing
When somebody who
sells you something talks
you into advertising the
same product to your
friends and relatives.
Voice Mail
Form of communication
where you can carry on a
conversation without
ever speaking directly to
the person you called.

Index

A

Acquisition, 185

B

bonus, 11, 54, 55, 57, 58
budgets, 28, 82
business location, 29
business lunch, 67

C

capital requirements, 14
centralized purchasing power, 150
cloning, 181
communication
    effective, 99
    verbal, 99
company structure, vi, 19, 71, 72,
    78, 178
computer, 91
    company system, 110
    hardware, 102
consensus Method, 78
corporate resources, 150
corporation, 4, 19, 20, 21, 22, 23,
    34, 57, 88, 135, 146, 150, 151,
    181, 189, 199
cost reduction, 70, 154

D

data explosions, 102
data handling, 103, 109
decision making, managers, 33
delegate, 94
de-merger, 178
discount, 57
disincentive, 60

summary, 61

E

E/S ratio, 153
e-mail, 71, 92, 93, 94, 95, 99,
    100, 101, 109, 121, 180
Employee
    effective, 150, 172
    supportive, 150, 171
enterprise system, 110
Environmental Service
    Department, 151

F

fads, 44, 52
financing, vi, 8, 85

G

government agencies, 116

H

Headquarter staff, 42
human factor, 150

I

Incentive
    group, 55
    plans, 54
    summary, 61
Incorporation (Inc.), 19
information age, 103
internet, 212
Internet, 23, 24, 25, 43
ISO 9000, 52
ITO, 38

L

Law of the Sphere, ii, v, vi, 51,
122, 138, 142, 164, 165, 167,
169, 170, 173, 174, 176, 178,
179, 187, 188, 192, 193, 194,
198, 204
   analytical use, 164
   definition, 166
   equation, 166
   military, 167
   ratio of effective to total
      employment, 170
   sales to profit ratio, 173
lawsuit, 80
leasing, 17
legal Entanglements, 13
Limited Partnership (Ltd.), 20

M

management layers, 144, 157
managing a company, 32
managing by committee, 69
manufactured goods, 24
Meetings
   domestic, 67
   informational or intruction, 68
   international, 75
   mania, 72
   what to do about, 78

N

non-profit contributing jobs, 61

O

operating expense requirements,
15
operating profit, 171
organizational charts, 41

P

phone tag, 98

power scaling factor, 128, 130,
131
product liability, 215
productivity gains, 103
proprietorship, 19
purchasing department, 36

R

R&D Department, 150
Reducing capital needs, 15
retail business, 23
Return on capital, 17

S

scaling factors, 127
ship-on-time, 58
software costs, 102
spending money, 62
staff requirements, 156
starting capital, 8, 14, 15, 16
starting capital, 18
state income tax, 30
system managers, 102

T

team, 73
team player, 180
teamwork, 78
telephone, 41
thermodynamics
   law of, 62

U

U.S. Army, 167
uniform financial reporting
   system, 180
United States Navy, 160

V

video conferencing, 100
voice mail, 41

Volkswagen Company, 168

W

wage differential, 154

web site, vi, 22, 23, 26, 44
word processing, 109